Legends, Lore & Lies

LEGENDS LORE & LIES

AUSTRALIANS AND THEIR DRIZA-BONES

CATHARINE RETTER

The Watermark Press

The legend of the bush.

® Driza-Bone is a registered trademark of Driza-Bone Pty Limited.

First published by The Watermark Press, Sydney

© Text 1992 Catharine Retter

National Library of Australia
Cataloguing-in-Publication data:
Retter, Catharine
    Legends, lore & lies: Australians and their driza-bones.

    Bibliography.
    ISBN 0 949284 19 X
    1. Coats. 2. Protective clothing. 3. Costume — Australia. I. Title.

391.00994

Produced by The Watermark Press, Sydney, Australia
Design and Picture Research — Susie Stubbs
Printed in China

To John Maguire for his intrepid faith.

CONTENTS

FOREWORD

As a small child growing up in the city, mad about horses, and with a love of the country that made the time between school holidays on friends' properties just stand still, one thing that brought the city closer to the country was Royal Agricultural Show time.

It is a time when the country comes to the city, but take Australian country dwellers out of the country and you can still tell they come from the bush. Whether you find them in their own domain among the cattle pavilions at the Show, downtown at the bank's head office, or on an annual shopping spree at David Jones or Myer you can pick them a mile away. You recognize them first by their attire, and it is said that one can even catalogue the size of a country person's property in inverse proportion to the width of the brim on their hat.

Unhurried, as those accustomed to the inevitability of Mother Nature and the knowledge that she is one part of life that cannot be hurried, their attitude and humour follow suit somewhat laconically.

A country person's personal space is larger than their city counterpart and when they shake your hand in greeting, they keep their distance, leaning towards you as one not only unaccustomed to, but also uncomfortable with the inevitable proximity of city crowds and shops and trains.

Typically the male country dweller is tall, long in the body, and usually looks good in moleskins (his city cousins rarely do), and when the hat is finally removed you are surprised by the white forehead which defines the area perpetually shaded from the harshness of the sun.

When you see him perched on the rail at the saleyards, watching his progeny at the local shows, or doing business down at the stock and station agent, the hand outstretched in greeting extends from a tweed jacket and finely checked shirt. The rural manager or property owner wears them loyally with a pure wool tie, a hand plaited leather belt and comfortable pure cotton moleskins. Elastic-sided leather boots complete the picture unless it rains, whereupon the man who spends his life outdoors would not venture out without his long oilskin coat.

That is the picture of the "bushie" who comes to town for the Royal Show. What you don't see so readily is his working attire. The battered and holey hat, the faded shirt (sometimes it is easier to remove the sleeves altogether than bother repairing them again), the multi-patched trousers or shorts and the heavy prickleproof socks above dusty boots. And in the rain, the ten or fifteen year old Driza-Bone with the odd rip, or with a leg or wrist strap long gone to God.

But there is much more to country dwellers than their appearance, for behind the laconic humour and the ubiquitous costume lie two centuries of toil and mateship. Finely interwoven with the threads of this way of life, and the spinning of a few good yarns down the years has emerged the story of the people, their mates and an oilskin coat that grew into a legend.

Dry As A Bone Days

As they drove them up the Barwon
Where the dust lay fetlock deep
They reminisced of younger days
Of spring, and rain, and lack of sleep,
and the barmaid in the pub up Walgett ways.

They'd seen their share of seasons
As they drove them up the Barwon
But today age called for Revenge not Reason
For the Drover's End up Walgett ways
burnt down last week.

And their throats like the season
Were parched and bare
And dry as sunstruck bones ...

C.J. Bergerac

The Legend of the Bush

Towards a National Costume

To the city dweller or the casual visitor in today's Australia it can be hard to imagine what the land was like before cities and expressways and urban sprawl. Even in the countryside with its endless, treeless, sheep populated paddocks it is difficult to conjure up a countryside completely covered in scrub so thick that a 30km journey to town to buy supplies would be a day long excursion. In those days the grey green eucalypts stretched as far as the eye could see and refused to die even in the face of drought and bushfires, until their lives were chopped short by those who owned them, into squat branchless stumps. And then there were the tangly, scrubby brush thickets that blocked your path and strangled the sparse fodder for the house cow and the work horses which those with a better start in life owned when they first faced the prospect of taming the bush. The home would be a rough hut beside which they would clear enough land to plant a paddock of wheat or run a few head of sheep.

The land called for the ability to survive hardship and the stamina to work the length of the daylight hours, six and seven days a week, year in, year out. And then start again because bushfire ravaged the crop before it was harvested, or the floods killed off the newborn lambs and

Removing a threshing plant with bullock dray, Yangan, Queensland, 1899.

most of the ewes, or the drought meant feed was so scarce you had to sell the flock you'd worked so hard over the past years to build up (if the sheep duffers didn't get them first).

What drove those early Australians to persevere and, as the country testifies today, to succeed against the hardship and the heartbreak? But then, what was the alternative? Months and months at sea and back to industrial England, where the cities had open sewers and overcrowded dwellings with their attendant epidemics? Where the only opportunities were to work the length of the daylight hours (and longer) in the factories, mills and mines? It was not much of a choice.

In Australia, you could work the land without having been born to it. In the bush there was hardly overcrowding or the threat of the spread of urban disease. Your health was your strength. And if you gave up the fight for a better life, there was the dread that you were also giving up the chance of a better life for your children.

The early squatters who took over the land became stamped with the mark of perseverance. They were not afraid of an honest day's work, and that stamp built something of a national character into their descendants. A characteristic for practicality, hard work, a caring for one's mates, and being a bit of a larrikin when it was time to relax.

To be in Australia then was to be in a country, and a time, that built the likes of Bert (B.J.) Facey whose outlook on the unimaginable hardships of his life led him to write his story as that of *A Fortunate Life*, and the cattlemen of the high country who are the inspiration for the legend of *The Man from Snowy River*, immortalised in Australian hearts by Banjo Paterson.

Their taste in housing was a reflection of the materials at hand which were usually the trees they felled as they cleared the land for crops and grazing. Their transport was Shank's pony, or if fortune had smiled on them, the four legged variety. For the man and woman on the land there were no long snowbound winter months which lent themselves to the intricate embroidery or fine woodworking of their European counterparts. Their lifestyle and their dress were, above all, practical. They had no time for the fanciful nostalgia of a national costume in the tradition of the Dutch farmers, the Greek peasants, the Russian folk dancers or even the kilted Scots.

Cooking with camp oven and billy.

A typical settler's hut at the turn of the century.

Moreover most national costumes seem to date from times when Australia did not even appear on the map. Certainly there are no national costumes based on modern Western clothes which are predominantly those of urban dwellers. Nor is there much difference between the Australian city dweller's costume and those of their European or American peers. The uniform of jeans, or suits and ties for the more businesslike is found all over the modern world.

Yet today we have more time for nostalgia and with it a return to country values which are perceived to be honest and wholesome. These have also brought about a resurgent interest in handicrafts and movies which romanticise the struggles of our early settlers. It is also the movie industry which has helped change Australia's modern perception of its claim to a national costume. Ironically, the movie that did so much to help this along was *The Man from Snowy River*. It showed a side of country life in Australia from earlier this century which is still reflected

in today's rural life. For in any country gathering there is bound to be a uniform or costume that is unmistakably Australian and predominantly male: an Akubra hat, moleskin trousers, short elastic sided boots, probably a finely checked shirt with flapped pockets and undoubtedly a Driza-Bone coat.

Twentieth century Australian women appear to have missed out on a traditional costume, perhaps because they followed changing fashions a little more than their men. But some aspects of clothing transcend the sex barriers. The ever practical Driza-Bone surfaces each year in the Wet, worn by man and boy, woman and girl alike. And the ubiquitous furfelt Akubra shades not only the heads of male and female in the long hours under the relentless sun but they say an Akubra's not really broken in until it has been dipped in the creek and the cooling water poured over the head of its wearer, or been filled to give a thirsty horse a drink.

Windjammer Days

The Driza-Bone coat began life on board the sailing ships which plied their trade along the so-called Roaring Forties. This was the name given to the belt of latitude between 40° and 50° in the Southern Hemisphere. It was at this latitude that the large sailing ships were able to travel fastest on account of the strong prevailing winds which blew, unhindered by any land mass, across the Southern oceans. Hard wearing and galeproof wet weather gear was an essential for the comfort, health and ultimately the survival, of the crews of these ships. And it was on board one of these fast-moving windjammers that a thrifty and enterprising young Scot with the distinctly un-Scottish name of E. Le Roy, discovered that torn windjammer sails had another life after being rent by the elements.

The windjammers brought out manufactured goods from Britain and Europe and took back wheat and wool. In those days wool needed to be transported at speed to ensure that it arrived in London in time for the wool sales. These were only held during the first three months of the year and when a ship arrived late it could mean the added expense of storing the cargo for another 10 months before it might be sold. This meant that the fastest ships were in great demand, especially as the time

OPPOSITE PAGE
Captain Corner of "Macquarie" and "Rodney" in 1882, modelling a forerunner of today's Driza-Bone.

Mending the sails.

drew closer to the sales. Initially the ships used for these voyages were the fast, sleek clippers, which were first used to bring tea back from China and then to carry wool from Australia. These ships were famous for their speed and names like *Cutty Sark* and *Thermopylae*, which did the London to Melbourne run in sixty days, have become part of seafaring lore.

But as fast as these ships were, they had the disadvantage that their freight capacity was insufficient to satisfy the expanded trade between Australia and Europe. In their place came the iron-hulled ships known as windjammers which had up to five masts, square rigging and acres of canvas stretched taut in the wind. Whereas the clipper ships were made of timber and had a natural buoyancy, these massive square hulled monsters charged on through the seas rather than riding over them.

When loaded, a windjammer had scarcely more than one and a half metres of freeboard (clearance above sea level) so that the decks were almost constantly awash. This meant that the crew actually lived in their oilskins coats, for even fair weather still meant constant spray and waves sluicing over them.

It was usually considered safer to be aloft in the rigging than on deck where any sailor risked being washed overboard by the massive waves that would sweep the length of the ship from bow to stern and on occasions from the other direction too. Nor was there much hope for any man washed overboard, since there was no way of stopping these flying, rust streaked mammoths, particularly in the stormy waters around Cape Horn.

For a sailor to go aloft, he would need to climb up the large netlike ropes called ratlines making sure that he started on the weather side. By so doing the wind would force him against the ropes rather than blowing him off. Once aloft, the hardest and most time consuming work was trying to furl sails in a high wind.

The crew, and at times it was the whole crew excepting the helmsman, would stand on a sagging footline while they bunched and tied the wildly flapping sails. This task was not always easily achieved as the ship heaved and yawed and the men gyrated from one extreme to the other. It was the skill of these few men fighting the elements in wind-blown, rain-swept oilskins that epitomised the windjammer days.

As a result of all this, the crews of the windjammers enjoyed a certain bravado brought about by constantly challenging the elements. For the size of these ships the crews were relatively small and always worked as a team.

Yet despite the daily exhaustion from working on these ships, E. Le Roy still managed to spend a little of his time thinking about and experimenting with his clothing project. He could indeed be considered an early exponent of recycling as with careful cutting and waterproofing he transformed torn sailcloth into workwear coats.

Aloft in the rigging, the crew furl the sails.

Putting into practice the scientific theory that oil and water don't mix, Le Roy waterproofed the canvas with linseed oil, beeswax and paraffin. The coats treated in this manner proved most effective when used by sailors at sea, where they were never stored away for long periods, for if it wasn't raining, they were being used against the wind and the spray. In the warmer latitudes, the same natural cotton canvas allowed the coats to breathe, thus minimising body heat condensation and the uncomfortable, personal "greenhouse" effect that is well known to the wearers of the modern day marvels of plastic and PVC raincoats.

Le Roy may have been working in isolation on the Southern Oceans but around the world at the same time other kindred spirits were at work inventing some of the things we take for granted today. Count von Zeppelin was launching his airships in Germany, Orville and Wilbur Wright were testing their heavier than air machine in the U.S.A. and a thoughtful cyclist in Northern Ireland called J.B. Dunlop, tired of jolting his way over the cobblestones, invented the pneumatic tyre.

ON THE LAND

THE REAL BEGINNINGS OF THE DRIZA-BONE

It is one of those ironies of history that when E. Le Roy decided on a life ashore sometime around 1890 he settled not in Australia but in New Zealand, and so it was that Australia's national rainwear first found its land legs across the Tasman in another country altogether.

A close personal friend of Le Roy's, Thomas Edwin Pearson (known far and wide as T.E.) was in the 'Cleanliness is next to Godliness' business, manufacturing the famous Pearson's Sand Soap. In 1890, when T.E. decided to become an early Kiwi emigrant to Australia he settled not in Bondi, like so many of those who followed him, but in the inner western Sydney suburb of Drummoyne. But this was only a temporary haven and soon after he moved again, to the aptly named Kangaroo Street, Manly.

From this attractive seaside suburb he travelled far and wide seeking out a larger market for his soaps in Australia. It was in the course of these journeys that he discovered that the reputation of Le Roy's recycled sails had already spread to the Australian squatters and settlers by way of the windjammer sailors. For it was these hardy people who, like Le Roy, had forsaken the uncertainty of the seas for the

OPPOSITE PAGE
"Thank God for the rain (and for my Driza-Bone.)"

Thomas (T.E.) Pearson.

fickleness of the land, who had brought the mantle of Driza-Bone to the country.

T.E. Pearson still crossed regularly to New Zealand to secure the last of the quickly disappearing fine sands for his Sand Soap, and it was on one of those trips that he brought back a consignment of coats from his old friend Le Roy. When he landed them in Australia he was amazed at how great a demand there was for the coats and he sold the entire stock in

T.E.'s wife Rose Pearson.

less than a week. The two of them quickly decided that the coats should be manufactured locally in Australia where a much larger market existed.

Thus a new and thriving enterprise soon mushroomed from a backyard shed in Manly. The house where the two friends started the company still stands, as does the backyard shed, not much bigger than 5m x 5m but now overgrown and disused.

The backyard shed where the first Driza-Bones were made, now disused and overgrown.

But for the Great Depression, Le Roy might have moved permanently across to Australia to join T.E. in the expanding business in Kangaroo Street. But times were hard and the prudent decision seemed to be for Le Roy to stay put in Auckland. Meanwhile T.E. carried on the business and was soon employing other members of the family while he travelled regularly to supply his far flung band of customers.

In the tradition of all successful marketers T.E. listened well to what his customers told him and then adapted the original coat to suit the change from their needs at sea to their needs ashore. In particular the coat was made longer so that the rain did not run into the wearer's boots, and at the same time generously covered their knees and lower legs while on horseback.

A further refinement was a fantail which was added in the back to spread over the saddle and protect the saddle leather (and the wearer's seat) from drenchings. Next came wrist straps which stopped the rain from dribbling up the arms while the wearers erected fences or built dwellings in bad weather. All suggestions that might improve the product were considered and if it was agreed that they were effective they would then be incorporated into the Driza-Bone design. Another such improvement was the introduction of leg straps which stopped the coat from taking off in high winds.

The coats in those days were never dyed and retained their worn canvas look, officially described as "dark field grey". The earth brown colour by which the Driza-Bone coats are widely known today is in fact a more recent adaptation that was first achieved by treating the cotton canvas with copper and ammonia.

One other major difference between life at sea and life on the land led to another essential change to the coat. During the long dry season on the land, the coats were stored away, and when the rains came their unfortunate owners found them hardened into the weird and wonderful, but inhuman shapes they had been stored in. When they tried to remould them to their own shapes the unbending coats cracked in protest and then succumbed to the first rains. The culprit was found to be the linseed oil so often used on cricket bats but quite unsuitable for clothing. This oil was quickly dropped from the waterproofing formula and new ingredients added that allowed the coats to be stored during the long, hot summers without becoming hard and stiff or cracking. Over the years, the formula has been refined, but the exact ingredients remain a well kept secret to this day.

Trade
Marks
£2.

FORM B.

1 6 AUG 1933 To be accompanied by seven copies
of Form C and five unmounted
representations of the Trade Mark.

COMMONWEALTH OF AUSTRALIA

The *Trade Marks Act* 1905–1922.

COMMONWEALTH
17 AUG 1933
PATENT OFFICE

APPLICATION FOR REGISTRATION OF TRADE MARK.

AMENDED PURSUANT TO THE PROVISIONS OF
REGULATION 34 (2) (a).

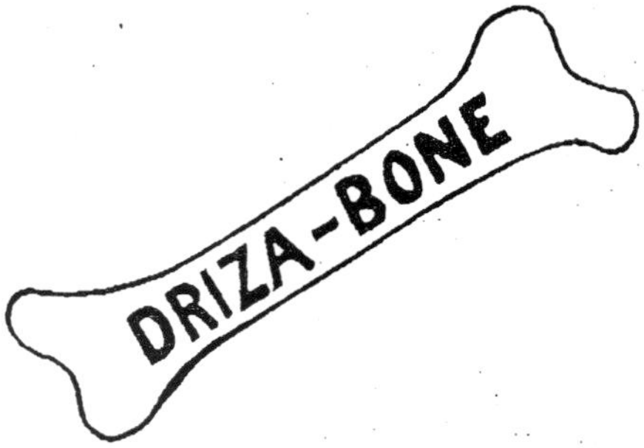

DRIZA-BONE

NEW SOUTH WALES
Fee 2/-
Time 2.20
Serial No. 12298
Date 16/8 1933

Art. Props: E. Le Roy (Aust) Pty. Ltd.

You are hereby requested to register the accompanying Trade Mark in

Class 38 , in respect of Waterproof Clothing comprising Ladies' & Gents' Raincoats and Golf Jackets, Gents' Riding Coats, Oilskin Pants, etc., Oilskin housing, leggings, Ladies' Skirts and gaiters, Children's rainwear,

in the name of Driza-Bone Clothing Company
6 Kangaroo Lane
Manly, Sydney, N.S.W.
Manufacturers

who claims to be the proprietor thereof.

My
Our address for service is 6 Kangaroo Lane,
Manly, Sydney, N.S.W.

Dated this 16th day of August A.D. 1933

DRIZA-BONE Clothing Coy

To the REGISTRAR OF TRADE MARKS,
Commonwealth of Australia.

One 'secret' ingredient in the early Driza-Bone days was a low flammable paraffin. T.E.'s grandson still remembers the day when T.E. took over the family kitchen to blend the waterproofing oils. In the tradition of small business improvisation, he borrowed a handy sized mixing pot (otherwise kept for making jams and preserves), found a conveniently empty spot on top of the stove and poured in the oils, stirring them together with a long handled wooden spoon.

Not far into his task the paraffin suddenly ignited from the heat of the slow combustion stove and T.E. was left with a blackened face, no eyebrows, a strong smell of burnt hair and an order banishing him from the kitchen for evermore.

Thinking of his customers sitting close to their campfires on chilly nights T.E. soon opted for a safer formula.

The business was now firmly established and T.E. and the family's thoughts turned to finding an appropriate name for their remarkable coat, a name that was neither Le Roy nor Pearson. T.E.'s grandson, Ray Pickup, recalls the day when his uncle the Reverend Bob Pickup (a nephew of T.E.) returned from his widespread parish rounds. Walking into the Kangaroo Street premises he immediately announced to the family that he had *found* the name. He then produced from behind his back a very large, and very sun-dried Hereford cattle bone. "You can call it 'Dry as a Bone'" he pronounced. There was unanimous agreement and a few days later the name "Driza-Bone" was formally registered by Le Roy and T.E., together with the traditional bone shape design.

Over the years the business was forced to move to larger premises, and apart from a short foray to T.E.'s weekender at Rooty Hill it remained in the Manly/Balgowlah area until the company was eventually sold by the family in 1974.

One of these premises, on the first floor of a building in Condamine Street still boasts the outdoor stairway so steep that it could almost be classified as a ladder. The fabrics had to be carried up in all

OPPOSITE PAGE
The original application to register the trademark Driza-Bone, dated the 16th August 1933.

weathers and the finished coats then had to be carefully carried back down. Older staff members recall they were often tempted to drop the lot from the top of the steps and pick them up again at the bottom.

T.E.'s grandson, Ray (now 70 himself), remembers grandfather Thomas as one of the world's true gentlemen in every sense of the word. He was gentle, a man of his word and a tireless worker who never felt the inclination to retire. He died at 96 years of age.

Ray also remembers meeting Le Roy's daughter in New Zealand some ten years ago, when she was 80 years old. Le Roy's Queen Street store in Auckland was long gone, victim, as so often happens, to failing family interest.

UP THE COUNTRY

Truth was, the hero of two districts had gone short on elementary education. Not that he was lacking in human skill or culture. He could glance at a forest giant and tell which way it would fall to his axe, and how many slabs it would yield to fashion his habitation. He could flay a beast and make from its hide harness and many other things. He could snare a wild horse and convert it into a domestic ally, as there was no outlaw wrapped in hide that could get rid of him while buckle and girth would hold. Nor was his love of horses rooted in gambling, but in personal friendship for a noble fellow-animal. He could canter over a stretch of country and estimate how many acres it contained, and how many beasts it would graze. He could make a fire in country girth-deep in snow or under pouring rain, and cook a meal at it. There wasn't a beast from the Upper Murray to the Lower Murrumbidgee that he didn't know by the cut of its jib, and no bird could call to its mate, nor outline its wing on the sky at dusk or dawn, without his reading it like the alphabet, and he could not be bushed while the stars shone at night or the sun by day, and when the sun failed the bark on the trees was a compass; but he would have thought all this what any duffer could do, and the fellow who could cover a sheet of paper quickly no end of a gun.

Brent of Bin Bin (Miles Franklin) *Up the Country*

*This illustration appeared in
the Autumn/Winter David
Jones catalogue of 1947.*

Sewing the Seams

Making the Coats

T hat Daddy of all Driza-Bones, the coat that was born at sea begat many generations of coats, all of which bore the strong family likeness.

At first they were bred in any colour as long as it was the colour of weathered sailcloth. Then, because most coats took on the colour of the mud splashes or the windblown dust of their surrounding countryside anyway, the official family colour became Earth Brown, for which it is widely known today.

The making of Driza-Bones and the wearing of Driza-Bones became so much a part of the extended Pickup family that the coat and its fabric infiltrated its way into every conceivable corner of their lives. Coats bearing the original Le Roy brand are still worn occasionally by the family and T.E. Pearson's grandson recalls all sorts of uses that the oilskin fabric was put to. Not only did they make Driza-Bone hats and bomber jackets from the fabric for their own use, but even swimming costumes and then an entire swimming pool. Children's tents and marquees for family picnic days were also cut and sewn by the seamers to house the growing band of T.E.'s descendants.

The original land cloth (found to be more reliable and longer lasting than recycled canvas sails) was an Egyptian cotton (a style of fabric, not a country of origin) and was woven in Scotland. The density of the weave was critical to its waterproofing qualities and the company's choice of fabric had much to do with the growing success of the coat. It is a quality T.E.'s grandson still swears by. He not only still has an old coat or two around the house made from the original land fabric, but proudly continues to demonstrate its toughness with a 'Driza-Bone' hood he made for his snow mobile in the same material and a handy cover for his favourite drill press in the shed.

To waterproof the fabric, back in the early years, it was laid out flat on the kitchen table and then later on a long purpose-built bench, and then hand-dressed with a rag dipped in the waterproofing formula. T.E.'s grandson recalls that it was about as exciting, and every bit as tedious, as polishing the family car every day of your working week. He was later saved from this laborious task by an ingenious drying contraption which blew steam in between two layers of a long table. There were rollers at each end of the table and in the middle was a trough filled with the waterproofing oils through which were winched the long bolts of fabric. Fortunately for today's workers, the oiling process is much less physically demanding and much more scientific with oil release gauges and temperature controls and a multitude of rollers to ensure an even distribution of the formula across the fabric.

From those early beginnings through to the 1970s the descendants of T.E. Pearson continued to run the family business. However, in the way of many families, and like Le Roy's descendants in New Zealand, most of the members had diversified their interests away from the family company until in 1974 they decided it was time to sell. By chance, one of the family went away on an ocean cruise aboard a P&O liner during which time he met the proprietor of the Armour safety clothing company. It just so happened that this gentleman was on the lookout for ways to expand his business. So the Driza-Bone company, which was in a sense founded at sea, had gone full circle, to be sold at sea to a new generation of owners.

Since 1974 the Driza-Bone company has changed hands once more and is now owned by the James Halstead Group, a company which has declared itself dedicated to the longevity of the Driza-Bone name and to upholding the traditions of Le Roy and T.E. Pearson for at least the next 100 years.

In the 1980s Driza-Bone moved with the times and expanded its product line into a range of colourful summerweight fabrics. Then, with Australia's new found nationalism and a demand for an internationally recognisable costume, Prue Acton, the designer for the Australian Olympic Team uniforms, asked Driza-Bone to create a coat in yellow as part of the 1988 team uniform for Seoul.

So widely acclaimed was Australia's striking Olympic uniform that it created a demand for an entire family of coat colours. The generation of bottlebrush-red Driza-Bones, bush green, sky blue, and navy in dry-oiled, summerweight coats began to be seen, particularly in the cities, alongside the more traditional browns and blacks.

The yellow Driza-Bone also inspired the creation of a children's version in safety yellow for school wear, and then a traditional mini version in Earth Brown for pony clubbers and traditionally-minded country kids.

It was the end of an era.

For as long as anyone born and bred in the country could remember, their childhood had been signposted with over-sized hand-me-down coats from older brothers and sisters, and even cut down versions of dad's old coats (when he became tired of searching high and low for his own coat on rainy days when one of the children got it before him).

The end of childhood was marked with the presentation of one's own full sized Driza-Bone. It was almost as though you had to earn the coat before you were considered big enough to wear one. Now, any kid can have his own coat. Gone is the tradition of the 21st birthday coat. Gone is the image of a coat bigger than its wearer.

The one tradition that hasn't disappeared though is the Hand-Me-Down, for the one drawback with kids' coats is that they seem to last years longer than the children who wear them. By the time the seven year old has grown to become a fourteen year old, his first coat has milked more cows, fed more chooks and gone to more pony club days than its original owner, because it has passed (along with the chores) to younger brothers, sisters, small neighbours and cousins.

Sneaking Dad's Driza-Bone is no longer necessary with the introduction of child size coats.

In the country, the Driza-Bone is essentially a work coat. You wear it when it rains or when it is cold, and when it stops raining you throw it where it lands. Whether this is the back of the ute, on the chair on the verandah, in the corner of the shed, or for particularly civilised and tidy types, on the hook on the back of the kitchen door. With this sort of treatment, the Driza-Bone was not always in a presentable state to wear to town or over to the neighbours for a Sunday barbecue, at least not without sidelong glances or averted noses. Yet it was such an institution and such a part of rural life, that Driza-Bone felt almost honour bound to bring out a weekend version, suitable for footy and the pub, or even a visit to the bank manager. From the mother of necessity therefore was born the Driza-Bone Brumby Jacket, complete with zip front, bomber jacket styling, handwarmer pockets and superfine lightweight water-proof cotton. This first major departure from the traditional caped oilskin coat proved a runaway success.

Prior to this bold departure from tradition, the cousins of the original Driza-Bone had been bred by processes of natural evolution. The change from horseback to motor car meant that there was room for a 3/4 length coat in the family, a coat which was more convenient for getting in and out of cars. Motorbikes, because of their closeness to the ground and their owners' tendency to plough willy nilly through paddocks whatever the height of the surrounding (wet) vegetation, required greater leg protection in all weathers. It was thus the Driza-Bone oilskin trousers came into being.

Meanwhile the ever increasing popularity of exploring the great Aus-tralian bush on foot inspired the development of another coat. This was a lightweight hooded coat for bushwalkers which occupied virtually the same space and weight as a pair of walker's socks in a backpack, the Driza-Bone Cyclone Coat.

In the 1990s, emboldened by the success of all these new coats, the range had become an extended family of oilskin, dry-oiled, cupra, moleskin and leather coats. Export markets demanded further innova-tions and in 1992, as a result of US and Japanese encouragement, the mid-length Driza-Bone Bushman's coat with zipped front and draw-string waist became a welcome addition to the range. Likewise, the Driza-Bone Swagman coats in Summerweight and Cupra came about as a result of interest from the European and U.K. markets.

Through this expansionary phase, Driza-Bone managed to do something that very few others achieve during times of increasing sales and production. They improved quality control, bought better fabrics and studs and increased their service standards to the saddlery outlets, tourist boutiques and clothing stores that were their main customers.

The home of Driza-Bone at Eagleby in Queensland is far from being a typical factory. The building had started life as an inn, and as a result came complete with numerous bathrooms and recreation areas. The bathrooms have been put to good use as testing rooms for new fabrics, seaming and waterproofing treatments. Prototype coats are dressed on dummies (real people can't be spared, although it has been threatened) and stood under the shower for up to eight hours at a time. At the end of the showers the dummies are thoroughly examined for the slightest signs of wettness from leaky fabrics or seams.

Two other areas important to quality control are seams and studs. In stress areas seams are double sewn and a time honoured tradition at Driza-Bone tests even the stoutest of seams (and hearts) and that is the challenge extended by the seamers to a tug of war with an innocent and unsuspecting Driza-Bone coat in the middle. With just pride in their workmanship, they like to issue the Challenge to the packers, cutters, quality control staff and even to the odd unsuspecting visitor. The result is a tug of war competition held on the lawn at High Noon, demonstrating the strength of their handiwork. Marquess of Queensberry rules are "strictly" adhered to with the Head of Despatch responsible for estimating body weights to establish teams of equal pulling power.

A stock and station agent in Minlaton in South Australia once cast doubt upon the claim that the fabric was virtually indestructible and, seeking some publicity for himself put some fabric in a vice and

Sewing the seams at the Driza-Bone factory in Eagleby.

unceremoniously tugged at it with pliers. The material refused to tear and he was soon forced to admit his defeat to the gathered media.

One of the quality tests that Driza-Bone sets most store by is the one performed by 'The Flasher'. This is the nickname handed on to each person who takes on the job of studs tester. With around eighteen pairs of heavy duty studs on the average coat, a failure rate of just 1 in 100 studs has the potential of ruining 1 in 6 coats. This would of course cause a most unacceptable rate of returns to the company and would quickly damage their unassailable image for toughness and reliability. The coat studs are therefore tested four times before they are approved.

We have it on good authority that The Flasher doesn't take his work home with him, but there was one Driza-Bone employee who did. In fact he lived and breathed Driza-Bone for over thirty years until he retired in 1984 at 96 years of age. The company seems to breed longevity amongst its long serving members. This person was Charles Knuckey, the South Australian agent for Driza-Bone who used to speculate that he had probably earned a place in the Guinness Book of Records as the world's oldest commercial traveller.

His territory was all of South Australia and at age 92 he bought himself a new Commodore car for his regular trips to Mt Gawler and beyond. At that time he had held a driver's licence for 70 years and, forced to sit a driving test annually, took pride in passing each time with flying colours. He kept outliving his cars he said, and had first learnt to drive in 1914 at which time he bought a motorbike that seemed to have a sense of direction all of its own. His first car, a two-cylinder Renault succeeded the bike in 1918.

Charles Knuckey was the epitome of a good salesman. He loved his product and selling Driza-Bones kept him young and interested. There was nothing that he couldn't tell you about the coats. Charles sold them to the South Australian Police, the highway workers and the Murray River punt and paddle boat operators as well as saddleries and menswear stores. The retailers on whom he called remember him fondly as bright, cheery, very genuine and with an excellent memory. "If he promised to do something for you, even in his 90s, you knew he would remember to do it."

A Gallipoli veteran, Charles Knuckey looked like a fit 65 year old and was bred of sturdy stock. His father and uncle were surveyors on the Queensland Overland telegraph lines and had braved Australia's roughest terrain, sickness, droughts and torrential rains. He was proud of being a reformed smoker for forty years and a vegetarian for thirty.

An avid Australian Rules footballer, his beloved South Adelaide Football Club returned his loyalty by naming their Best and Fairest Player

trophy for him. He used to joke that they were all waiting for him to die so that they could call it the Charles Knuckey *Memorial* Trophy.

Driza-Bone, Australian Rules and Nora, his wife of 63 years, were his life. He gave up involvement with the first two when Nora became ill and nursed her until she died. Colleagues say he lost the will to live after that. Charles Knuckey's photograph has a special place in the Driza-Bone museum at Eagleby, and his ideals live on in the company.

THE DRIZA-BONE MUSEUM

OLD DRIZA-BONES NEVER DIE...

Just a few years ago an old bushie walked into the Driza-Bone premises wearing an old Driza-Bone coat that even at first glance appeared to be about as old as he was, and probably a shade more dilapidated. He asked if he could get the coat re-oiled as it was starting to let in a bit of rain, but other than that he thought it still had a good few years in it.

According to the Driza-Bone people they thought it was the oldest coat, still in use, that they had ever come across. Made in the days when the official colour for Driza-Bones was still 'weathered sailcloth', there was a rip in the fabric that extended from just under the arm almost down to the hem. All the staff came in to marvel at the age of the coat and to have a yarn with its owner. When they tried to establish the age of both, the old man told them that as he was now getting on for seventy and had purchased the coat when he was still a pup (in his twenties) it must have been sometime during the 40s that he bought it.

He had some tales to tell about where he and his Driza had been. Mainly droving out west, he reckoned it had outlived a few of his horses, and even one or two of his mates. It had stuck by him longer than his missus and kept him a good deal warmer than she ever had, he said.

The Naryilco muster in 1936 employed 42 men and 146 horses.

At first the Driza-Bone people offered to re-oil the coat for him, the original oil having worn off long ago, and while he was there they would get one of the seamers to mend the rip under the arm. No, he didn't think that was necessary, just a re-oiling would do. Then because Driza-Bone were so impressed with his story, they suggested to him that perhaps it was time to give the coat an honourable resting place in the little Driza-Bone museum they had recently started up on the premises. They offered to replace his old coat with a brand new one if he would give them his old one for the museum.

Well, you would have thought they had tried to steal his most treasured possession or threatened to cut off a limb! He would have none of it, no new coat, no stitching up, just re-oiling thanks, "And I'll wait".

He made himself comfortable in a nearby chair and one of the women made him a cup of tea. One or two of the others chatted to him about his life in the bush, and he began to relax a little, basking in the female attention.

After a little while, one of the men ventured back with a brand new coat, just completed, and asked the old man if he would like to try it on while he waited and tell Driza-Bone what he thought of it.

The old man gave the younger one a bit of a sideways glance and the hint of a gruff smile, realising what he was up to, but went along with it and tried the coat on. He walked up and down, fastened the leg straps on, turned up the collar, adjusted the wrist straps once or twice. He sat back down in his chair and took another sip from his second cup of tea. He looked at the women and at their smiling approval, and with a resigned smile agreed that maybe it was time he got himself a new coat with studs that did up everywhere and with leg straps that were securely in place… but only if his old coat really was given an honourable resting place in the museum.

He left them then, and his parting promise was that he'd be back in about thirty years, to get the new one re-oiled… and to check up on his old mate in the museum.

The fire and floods test

On another occasion, a parcel arrived at the Driza-Bone offices with a letter from T.N. Gorman of Queanbeyan. He enclosed two of his older coats for repairing and redressing and if Driza-Bone could let him know how much it cost, he would send them the money. The two coats were both judged to be immediate post war models, made when the rationing restrictions were first lifted. Thinking that there might be an interesting tale or two attached to their lives, Driza-Bone phoned Mr Gorman instead of writing to him to let him know the cost of the repairs and the re-oiling.

T.N. Gorman was impressed with the promptness of Driza-Bone's response to his letter (it had taken *him* a few years to actually get around to sending the coats in, so it was indeed a swift response). The Driza-Bone caller and T.N. fell into conversation about the coats and T.N.

recalled putting one of the coats to a test at which even the Flasher or the Tug of War Brigade at Driza-Bone would have baulked.

T.N. recalled the time a bushfire was raging not too many miles away from the Gorman homestead, it had reached the neighbour's boundary

fence and T.N. was out on his horse moving his cattle well away from the path of the fire. His young sons had been told to stay around the family home and to keep the roof of the main building wet in case the wind changed and the fire headed for the homestead.

T.N. had managed to get the bulk of his herd to safer pastures and was looking for strays in the scrub when he realised that the fire had indeed changed course and his retreat was cut off. He set his horse loose, thinking it was better to let the animal fend for itself, then threw himself in a nearby ditch, covering himself from head to foot with his Driza-Bone. Even years later, in recounting the story, he still vividly remembered the emotions he went through in not knowing whether he would survive the fire and whether he would ever see his family again. The heat was intense and it was difficult to breathe, but the fire eventually passed over him. He was able to get up after his ordeal, neither he nor his Driza-Bone appearing much the worse for wear and then faced a long walk home, much of it over ground that was still hot underfoot.

There was no sign of his horse but he hoped that, unburdened by a rider, it had been able to outrun the fire. Two days later a weary, footsore stockhorse turned up at the gate leading to the house paddock, neighing for attention and a feed.

T.N. still marvelled at the toughness of his old coat, not only did it survive, he recalled, but it remained waterproof as well.

And as if to prove a point he told of another time when the river burst its banks and he and the boys (a few years older then) had been moving the cattle to high ground and then, cut off by the rising waters, they faced the prospect of sitting out the floods with the cattle for a few days or swimming back across the river. They decided on the latter. They knew the river well, it was not fast flowing and they judged they could swim across it safely with the horses. The bigger problem was the weather. It was miserably cold, their clothes would be soaked through in the crossing and they then had a long, cold and wet ride home.

With more bravado than he felt, T.N. told the boys to follow his example and take off all their clothes. He bundled everything up in his Driza-Bone, then holding on to his horse's saddle with one hand, and balancing his floating bundle with the other hand they swam the freezing river. Once on the opposite bank they climbed back into their bone dry clothes and made for home, with nary a sneeze or a wheeze between them!

The Arthur Stanley Coat

The durability of the Driza-Bone coat has often meant that its original owner outgrows it and the coat is handed down to a younger family member or a deserving neighbour. Sometimes fate steps in and relegates the Driza-Bone to the back shed come Christmas time when a well meaning relative gives its owner a new Driza-Bone even though there are still good years left in the first.

One such coat finished its days at the Driza-Bone museum in 1990 having had three different owners, all neighbours, and three rich and full lives. At Driza-Bone it became known as the Arthur Stanley coat and although he was not its first owner, his custodianship was probably the longest.

The coat first came into Arthur's possession before the Second World War, some time around the late thirties. He wore it to work for many years at the local abattoirs and he reckoned it saw a fair share of blood and guts as well as grease from the machinery. A good hose down and it was as good as new and ready to wear bushwalking at weekends. Arthur and the coat hiked the remote reaches of the Great Dividing Range until the War got in the way. The old coat then had a bit of a holiday for a few years, but after the War was dragged from its resting

place, dusted off and pressed into willing service whenever it rained or whenever the wind howled around the mountains (which was most of the time).

The coat had been given to Arthur by his neighbour, a gentleman called Owen Spencer Evans. Known to everyone as Owen, and known to his family as a bit of a black sheep, he had put the old Driza-Bone through years of good service in many parts of New South Wales before it was handed down to his friend and neighbour. He had worn it jackarooing and rabbiting and had used it to protect his clothing in all sorts of work.

The story of Owen Evan's Driza-Bone was traced through his daughter and son-in-law, now living in Sydney and both very much a part of the early history of the city. Son-in-law Brian is a familiar figure around the historic area of the southern end of the Sydney Harbour Bridge known as the Rocks wearing a historic policeman's uniform he walks the tourist beat. A walking encyclopaedia on Australia's history Brian is not past posing with tourists for photographs, providing directions and has also been known to arrest unsuspecting tourists for wearing dresses above their knees!

Owen's daughter, Joanna, also part of the Rocks, and the proud owner of a red Driza-Bone as part of her official Rocks Walking Tours uniform, recalled that her grandparents had great expectations that Owen would continue in the family tradition of either law or medicine, but Owen's first and only love was the land. He turned his back on the career his family had mapped out for him and went off to work on a sheep station in the prime wool country of the southern highlands of New South Wales. The first purchase he made out of his pay was a new Driza-Bone coat. Buying it meant he virtually had to do without until next pay but he reckoned it was more important to survive the southern gales than eat and be merry. Owen wore that coat constantly through freezing winters, through shearing seasons, through lamb marking and through hard times as he put himself through courses so that he could better his knowledge of the land.

His oilskin followed him to work at Dekyvere's, a famous Sydney woolbroking company where he became a wool classer, and then finally when he needed a new Driza-Bone fit for client meetings, his trusty Driza was given a new home next door, with neighbour Arthur Stanley.

More than forty years later, that same Driza-Bone was handed down to Arthur Stanley's son who, as an active scout, needed something that could be relied upon to keep the rain out during his bush hikes. The coat eventually found its way back to the local Driza-Bone retailer for re-waterproofing and when it arrived back at the factory its rightful place was judged to be the Driza-Bone museum.

Arthur Stanley was happy for his friend to spend the rest of its days in the hallowed luxury of a museum and he finished up buying three extra coats, one for each of his children. He bought Summerweights for each of them, ironically for the sole purpose of skiing and hiking in the Snowy Mountains. In the knowledge that it is better to dress in layers for cross country skiing and hiking, they found the lighter weight coats

The aptly named Charlie Winter takes Driza-Bone to the ski slopes at Lake Louise in Canada.

easy to fold up and carry in backpacks. The coats soon proved themselves in the rain and in the mountain's windy conditions offering the same full length protection as the traditional Driza-Bone. Their most recent foray was from Perisher up to the Summit and the Stanleys plan to give their coats a full and adventurous life before they in turn might qualify for residency at the museum.

The Word Had Passed Around

From Roustabout to Royalty

In the early days, Le Roy and Pearson sold their coats directly to their customers on the land, and while wet weather meant boom business it also made it a slow business moving around the country on unsealed roads which turned to mud in the wet.

So, in time, rather than selling their product directly to the farmers, they began to sell to retailers like the woolbrokers and stock and station agents such as Goldsborough Mort and Dalgety, who soon became their biggest customers. By then the name and reputation of Driza-Bone had spread widely and it was fast becoming the accepted name for raincoats in the Australian bush.

Those great emporiums, David Jones in Sydney and Myer in Melbourne, to which country families make annual pilgrimages, began selling the coats in the early 1940s. They also did a roaring trade on Driza-Bone's behalf, both in the store and through their biannual mail order catalogues.

Such was the versatility and usefulness of the Driza-Bone riding coat that advertisements for Driza-Bones appeared in the Spring/Summer

David Jones catalogue illustration, 1949-50.

Rain at the Sydney Royal
Easter Show.

edition as well as the Autumn/Winter edition of the David Jones catalogues each year.

Apart from these outlets, each year when the farmers came to town for the annual Royal Show, the Driza-Bone company set up its own stall at the Showgrounds and sold their coats as quickly as the factory in Manly could cut them out and sew them up.

Inevitably over the years the reputation of the Driza-Bone coat became widely known. Renowned for so many years in the bush for its practicality and many clever features, its fame continued to spread until slowly but surely city dwellers too were let in on the secret.

Perhaps the city folk saw the Driza-Bones first at the annual Royal Agricultural Show, or maybe it was when visiting friends in the country, or perhaps they admired a dapper bushie striding past on one of his rare visits to town.

Somehow, along the way we all got to hear about them and it soon followed that Australians adopted the Driza-Bone as part of a developing national costume and as an Australian icon. It was something unique which had been with us for as long as anyone could remember and which reflected the ingenuity and practicality of our pioneer beginnings.

The name Driza-Bone is described in *Brands*, a book on world famous brands, as "a name so thoroughly Australian, it even has to be said with an Australian accent".

Australia remains the land of opportunity in comparison to the larger, longer settled countries in the northern hemisphere, even if the opportunities these days are often snapped up by international developers. So it is befitting that one of the symbols of Australia's identity, the Driza-Bone coat, is something that can be purchased regardless of wealth, and worn regardless of status. It is ironically both a work coat and increasingly a fashion item, yet the statement it makes about its wearer is one of down-to-earth practicality.

With its growing identification as part of an Australian national costume it is not surprising that the Driza-Bone has started to make an appearance on occasions when a national costume and identity is required. Indeed nowadays many Australians representing their country wear a Driza-Bone coat in Australia or while on tour throughout the world.

Traditionally the coat is worn by Australia's Rugby Union team (the Wallabies) and Rugby League team (the Kangaroos) on their world tours; by touring Australian Test Cricket teams and by the Australian Equestrian Team when they ride at the World Championships.

LET IT RAIN...LET IT POUR...
you'll be dry-as-a-bone in your

DRIZA-BONE

SUPERFINE LIGHTWEIGHT RIDING COAT

You'll get complete protection from the weather in this popular superfine lightweight riding coat. Cut in full style, allowing perfect freedom and comfort of movement. Driza-Bone features a wide shoulder cape and fan-tail back, storm cuffs, leg straps, double front, reinforced sleeves and saddle lining. And you'll get years of wear from Driza-Bone. It's made from mildew-resistant cotton and guaranteed not to stick or crack. Try on Driza-Bone today.

SIZES 5-7
$23.95 £11/19/6

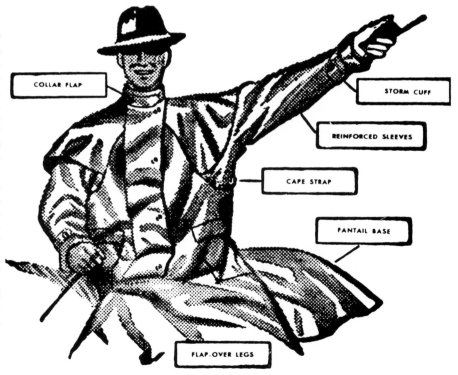

COLLAR FLAP

STORM CUFF

REINFORCED SLEEVES

CAPE STRAP

FANTAIL BASE

FLAP-OVER LEGS

Teams as diverse as the Australian Coarse Fishing Team have been warm and dry in competition on the banks of rivers here and overseas, and although Australia's Sky Diving Team at Barcelona didn't go quite as far as throwing themselves out of the aeroplane in their Driza-Bones they stopped crowds there during the World Championships nonetheless.

In 1988 our Australian Olympic Team marched proudly into the stadium in Seoul for the opening ceremony of the XXIVth Olympiad wearing bright yellow Driza-Bones and waving Akubra hats. A sporting and fashion success at the Seoul Games, the coats were made specially at the request of fashion designer Prue Acton who said at the time "If an Australian in a Driza-Bone walks down the street in New York, everyone turns and looks, because it's got a certain glamour about it."

But it is not only Australian teams who like to wear Driza-Bones as part of their outfits; the 1989 British Lions Rugby team sported the coat on their tour Down Under and racing drivers on the U.K. circuit seek out Driza-Bone for sponsorship so they can justifiably wear the coat when an opportunity arises.

1991 saw both the Oxford and Cambridge rowing crews wearing Driza-Bones for luck (which worked for one team, if not the other) prior to their annual boat race. Most recently, in 1992, on its historic World Cup tour the South African Cricket Team wasted no time in asking for the coat previously inaccessible to them through world trade embargoes.

Our pride in the Driza-Bone coat has also made it a favoured gift to official visitors to Australia, and very popular with the recipients. In 1988 the year of Australia's Bicentenary celebrations and also the year that Brisbane hosted the World Expo, Driza-Bone sales reached what was then an all time high. The coat was proudly worn by all the international Expo Commissioners and Driza-Bones were given to VIP visitors from all over the world. Presentations of the coats were made

OPPOSITE PAGE
This advertisement appeared in the Dalgety-N.Z.L Merchandise Service Guide in 1966, the year Australia's currency changed from pounds and pence to dollars and cents. On another page instructions show the correct way to write dollars and cents.

On the sponsorship trail.

to the Duke and Duchess of Kent; the Duke and Duchess of York; to the Japanese Prime Minister, Noboru Takeshita, and his wife Naoko; and to the British Prime Minister Margaret Thatcher and her husband Dennis.

That year, amid the patriotic fervour of the Bicentenary, Australia's Prime Minister, Bob Hawke, was photographed wearing a Driza-Bone on Australia Day. The Driza-Bone museum also boasts an autographed photo of an earlier Prime Minister, Malcolm Fraser, wearing a Driza-bone while riding a horse.

Other famous visitors to our shore who had to have a Driza-Bone were Nancy and Ronald Reagan (black coats with an ink blue lining) and entertainer Liberace who ordered 17 for his entourage and two for himself (one in puce and one in maroon).

Perhaps the best recommendation though comes from members of the British royal family who have been spotted wearing coats with the Driza-Bone cut. Prince Charles appeared on the cover of Country Life magazine in 1991 striding along in a trusty oilskin, while Fergie made the news showing her "country chic" at a shoot near Sandringham, matching her coat with rabbit fur trimmed wellington boots. Princess Anne brought coals to Newcastle when she wore hers as part of her British Horse Society uniform when they toured Australia in 1986.

The increasing popularity of Driza-Bone among overseas visitors led the company to the answer to a problem that had dogged them since World War II. At that time coat sales, like dew in a drought, dried up overnight.

Fabric supplies were diverted to soldiers' uniforms and other mysterious military purposes, and the Driza-Bone men like so many others went off to fight for King and country. Somehow though the company managed to stay in production during the war years despite shortages of both staff and materials. It was not until fabric restrictions were lifted after the war that the company was able to begin producing oilskins again in any numbers.

The war however was a quite different problem to the one which beset the company on a much more regular basis, and that was drought. In Australia, as in many countries, the dry years come with amazing regularity, occasionally lasting for three to five year cycles, and a raincoat in a drought is about as useful as a hole in a waterbag or a wooden leg in a bushfire. How then to weather the dry years and be ready for the wet? Should the company diversify?

Stubbies had the workwear market sewn up. Speedo had cornered the summer market in swimwear and Akubras, synonymous with hats in Australia, were worn come hail or shine. The big question for the Driza-Bone company was how to develop new products for the local market that would be complementary to their existing product lines yet capture sufficient market share.

NEW YEAR 1991 £1·60

COUNTRY LIVING

PORTRAIT OF THE PRINCE

By Patten, Porritt and others in the know

IT'S SO BRACING!
Midwinter swimmers crack the ice

DO YOU FIND IT HARD TO SLEEP?

NFU UNDER FIRE
Farmers fight back

THE CELTS ARE COMING

Decorating with paisley

Festive Irish feasts

Ghostly castles

Plaids and lassies

DERVLA MURPHY · EDWARD HEATH · JEANINE McMULLEN

Driza-Bone realised they would have to solve the problem of the seasonality of their products with some lateral thinking. The seemingly obvious but overlooked solution was for the Driza-Bone company to develop its markets on the other side of the globe, where the seasons were in reverse, and where wet winters seemed to be the norm just when El Nino was causing the Big Dry Down Under.

It was around this time that the Australian film *The Man from Snowy River* appeared. This beautiful film which was shot in the rugged mountainous country of the Southern Alps was based on the famous poem by Banjo Paterson. The film, which starred Kirk Douglas, Tom Burlinson and Sigrid Thornton, featured many riders wearing Driza-Bone style coats (though the poem was actually written when the father of the Driza-Bone coat, E. Le Roy was still at sea). Seen by millions internationally the film generated great interest in Australia and all things Australian.

Famous bushman R.M. Williams was one of the first to realise the export potential of the Driza-Bone coat. Normally a retail customer of

OPPOSITE PAGE
His Royal Highness, Prince Charles walks around a royal estate wearing his oilskin coat.

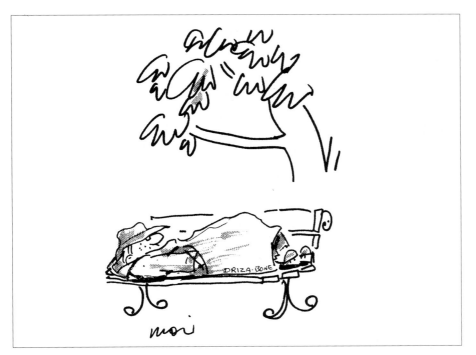

Cartoonist Alan Moir sees the funny side of Australia's assault on London's high street.

Driza-Bone, he began selling the coats in America, as an exporter. R.M. thinks he was probably also one of the first to recognise the coat's fashion potential and recalls that his export efforts resulted in the listing of Driza-Bone in a New York fashion magazine within a select group of products that were given the official status of being 'in' that year.

By the early 1990s Driza-Bone's own export efforts were beginning to pay handsomely and they saw sales grow to represent 30% of the company's total. Coats for the U.K., America, Japan, Argentina, Uruguay, South Africa, Germany, Holland, France, Italy, Ireland, New Zealand and Zimbabwe are all made at the Eagleby factory in Queensland.

PIONEERS

They came of bold and roving stock that would not fixed abide;
They were the sons of field and flock since e'er they learned to ride;
We may not hope to see such men in these degenerate years
As those explorers of the bush — the brave old pioneers.

'Twas they who rode the trackless bush in heat and storm and drought;
'Twas they that heard the master-word that called them further out;
'Twas they that followed up the trail the mountain cattle made
And pressed across the mighty range where now their bones are laid.

But now the times are dull and slow, the brave old days are dead
When hardy bushmen started out, and forced their way ahead
By tangled scrub and forest grim towards the unknown west,
And spied the far-off promised land from off the ranges' crest.

Oh! ye, that sleep in lonely graves by far-off ridge and plain,
We drink to you in silence now as Christmas comes again,
The men who fought the wilderness through rough, unsettled years
The founders of our nation's life, the brave old pioneers.

A.B. Paterson

ON THE TRACK

PRESERVING AUSTRALIA'S OUTBACK HERITAGE

In the 1970s one of Australia's far sighted bushmen, the renowned R.M. Williams, realised that there was a part of Australia's heritage that would soon disappear for all time under the ever increasing urban expansion unless steps were taken to preserve it. His aim was to preserve pioneering routes, early stock routes, bullock trails and gold mining settlements. The places where Australia's recent history was made. Just in the way that museums preserve and display the artefacts of a country's history, he saw the need to preserve where and how our history unfolded so that future generations could recapture the beauty of the landscape and also appreciate the conditions which the pioneers faced in their drive to settle the great land.

R.M. Williams is known not only for his famous brand of elastic sided riding boots which he started making in 1934, but also as the inspiration behind the Stockman's Hall of Fame, Hoofs & Horns magazine, the Tom Quilty Cup, the Rough Riders' Association and more. He also founded what was to become the 5,330km Bicentennial National Trail, a trail for bushwalkers and horse riders alike, stretching from Cooktown and the Daintree Rainforest in north Queensland, through the vast remote cattle country of New South Wales, and along the rugged beauty

OPPOSITE PAGE
The southern end of the National Trail at Healesville near Melbourne is marked by a monument.

of the stock route which wanders through the Guy Fawkes National Park. It closely follows the rivers and gorges of the Demon Fault line, picks its way through the well cared for horse trails of the Australian Capital Territory and rediscovers the home of the mountain horsemen of the Snowy Mountains. It then winds its way down into dense forests, past the trout-filled rivers and sub-alpine meadows of Victoria to its final destination, Healesville.

In 1973, R.M. Williams convinced a young and energetic horseman named Dan Seymour to ride the proposed trail to establish the best continuous route for its entire length. With his blue cattle dog and two horses Dan Seymour blazed a trail through the countryside, it took him two years and wherever possible he followed the original trails used by the pioneers, the stockmen and even the bushrangers of our past. He followed routes used by bullock wagons to cart provisions to far flung settlements, skirting cattle stations which still exist. He travelled through gold mining settlements, once throbbing with life and wealth but now resembling ghost towns reminiscent of those in wild west movies. His journey took him along the route of the first telegraph lines where many of the poles remain, standing like silent memorials to our modern communication network. He wound the Trail through National Trust classified towns, past the relics (rapidly being overgrown by the encroaching bush) left by tens of thousands of Chinese people who arrived during the gold rushes of the last century and where today's Trail walkers still fossick for their fortunes. He followed the route taken by the explorer John Oxley and also traced some of the historic trails of the Cobb and Co. coaches in Queensland and parts of northern New South Wales.

Names still in use along the Trail indicate earlier incidents in the life of the countryside. In one stretch of the bullock route there is a hill named "Wine for Dinner Hill", named after a long forgotten bullocky whose cart lost a wheel while straining up the hill. The cart, unbalanced, lost part of its load including a cask of wine which split open as it hit the ground. The bullocky, a sensible soul, realised that there was little he could do to save the wine and that it was destined to run to waste in the brown earth unless he rescued it in anything he could lay his hands upon. He quickly spread his Driza-Bone upon the ground under the cask to catch the run off and scooped up whatever else he could into his pannikins and mugs. Lying on a corner of his Driza-Bone he surveyed his domain and had "wine for dinner" for the rest of the day.

Part of the Queensland section of the Bicentennial National Trail.

A map showing the route of the Bicentennial National Trail as it winds its way down the east coast of Australia. Longreach the site of the Australian Stockman's Hall of Fame is also marked.

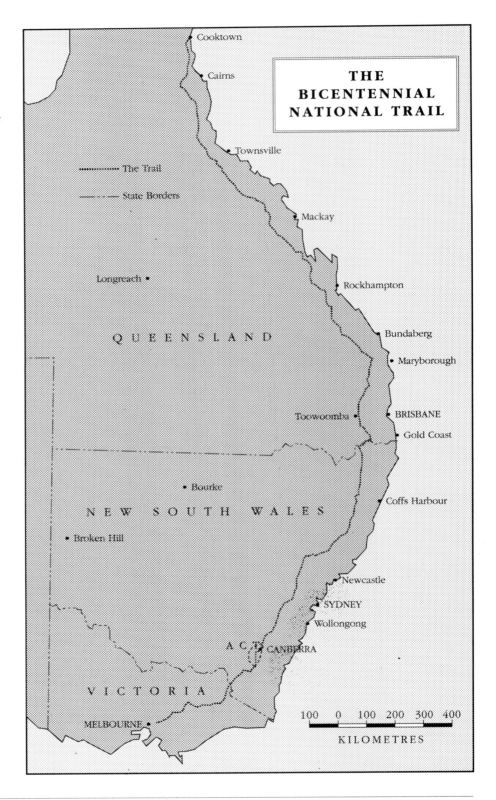

THE BICENTENNIAL NATIONAL TRAIL

Cooktown

Cairns

Townsville

•••••••••• The Trail

—·—·— State Borders

Mackay

Longreach •

Rockhampton

Bundaberg

• Maryborough

QUEENSLAND

Toowoomba • • BRISBANE

Gold Coast

• Bourke

Coffs Harbour

NEW SOUTH WALES

• Broken Hill

Newcastle

SYDNEY

Wollongong

A.C.T. CANBERRA

VICTORIA

MELBOURNE •

100 0 100 200 300 400

KILOMETRES

Today, in support of R.M.'s vision and in recognition of the people who opened up the land, Driza-Bone is a sponsor of the Bicentennial National Trail.

The pioneering spirit of the people who live along the route of the Trail remains, and to ride or walk the Trail is to experience a long line of encounters with some of the most colourful of Australia's bush characters. The more remote the areas of the Trail, the greater the individuality of the people.

There are old bushies in the back blocks of the National Trail with five days growth on their faces, baling twine holding up their baggy trousers, and tie wire lacing their boots. Their unpretentious dwellings are chock full of a lifetime's collection of things they couldn't bear to throw away, except in the kitchen, which is kept reasonably free from their collectables, for this is the room in which they live. Typically, the smoke from the wood burning stove has stained the walls and ceiling, the fly paper hanging from the light has been there since 1972, and beside the couch against the far wall is eighteen months' supply of *Queensland Country Life* newspapers.

Out back on the verandah sits a curly straw broom next to an assortment of old boots in various states of disrepair and a rough tumble of split firewood for the stove. On the wall on a rusty nail hangs an old bridle (repaired with more tie wire) and beside it on another nail a thirsty old Driza-Bone hangs forlornly, leg straps long gone. The steps off the porch are greyed with age, and the second bottom step is always missing.

Back in the kitchen you choke from the smoke, but the dwelling's owner doesn't seem to notice it at all. If you can last long enough, these old blokes have a few good yarns to tell the occasional passer-by. After a lifetime of living and working in the bush they have become as much a part of it as the trees by the porch. Time is immaterial, and their isolation means they have suffered little from the social pressures to conform to what are, anyway, sometimes doubtful social values.

There is one old tin scratcher at the Lion's Den Pub, up near Cooktown at the northern point of the Trail. No, he'd never married, he drawls. "I couldn't see the point in givin' away half me tucker just to get the other half cooked for me."

His eating habits are probably much like the wizened old fellow who makes an occasional trip to Gloucester on a New South Wales stretch of the Trail. He treats himself to a counter lunch at the pub when in town.

"Steak and onions please, love" is his standard request on these rare visits.
"Certainly sir, with vegetables or salad?" comes the reasonable response.
"None of that fancy stuff, just steak and onions" is the gruff reply.

Most of the people you meet in the bush are there simply because that is where they earn their living. Many were born and bred there, and continue the work of their parents. But an increasing number of newcomers seek the bush life out of a refusal to accept the pressures of city life and city expectations. Some, reminiscent of the swagman of yesterday, choose to live in the most inaccessible places just to avoid contact with society.

Regardless of their reasons for being there, most share a love and respect for their environment that is sometimes difficult to find in the cities. Change is rarely welcomed in the bush, and a few of these characters have taken exception to the idea of horseriders and bushwalkers entering their expansive domain.

One such character, who lived along an old stock route that is part of the Trail was very ready to list the catastrophes that would befall 'his' valley if city folk discovered the Bicentennial National Trail. By the time he had gone through the prospect of gates being left open, campfires getting out of control and burning all his paddocks, and motorbike riders terrorising his stock, he was becoming a bit worked up.

Getting redder and redder in the face with each breath he continued through weed infestations, litter blowing all around the place, walkers getting lost and needing rescue. Finally, at a point where he looked fit to burst, he came out with "Them druggies will have the place covered in marijuana, and the next thing you know all the cows'll have AIDS and they'll never get in calf."

Five years later, his cows still haven't caught AIDS and the nearest the Trail comes to his property is along a public right of way, a surveyed but unmade road. He's come to accept the inevitability of the occasional traveller but is still waiting for his fears to materialize.

When the National Trail was first being surveyed in minute detail so that its route could become officially recognised and guidebooks written for future trekkers, the organisers worked closely with National Parks and Wildlife, the Forestry Commissions and other experts in the field. On one occasion, at the suggestion of the National Parks Service, Mike Allen the Trail Co-ordinator was surveying an alternate section of the route which circumvented a national park but which was some fifty kilometres longer. He recalls an unexpected encounter,

"The first time I met Peter I was looking down the barrel of his gun, and he was stroppy. Real stroppy." What National Parks had omitted to tell Mike was that the alternate route went right through the middle of Peter's property, and he was not inclined towards visitors.

Peter lives at the end of a long road up in the mountains, two hours' drive from the nearest town. A veteran of the Malaya campaign, disillusioned by his fellow man, he found his haven as far away from people as he could get. All he wanted was a peaceful existence raising cattle but his life was a constant battle against 'the Authorities', council regulations, the Tax Office, Medicare and now the National Parks which wanted bits of his precious land to add to the adjoining Park. He fought them over the fires he claimed they couldn't or wouldn't control, and over the pigs and dingoes that came out of the park into his property. He fought with everyone who wouldn't leave him in peace.

A group of stockmen photographed at their temporary camp.

Any smarties in four wheel drives or on motorbikes who tried to follow the fire trail beyond the end of the road were usually dissuaded by a shot or two aimed over their heads. A bit of fast talking by Mike resulted in Peter lowering the rifle and letting him on his way.

It wasn't until a subsequent visit, when Mike had to face the prospect of encountering him again (he had practised his fast talking for days beforehand) that he had the chance to talk to him at length and learn a little about him. It turned out that, like many in the bush, he read and absorbed every printed word he could lay his hands on and was quite knowledgeable on an extraordinary range of topics.

He had firm views on economics and politics and wasn't afraid to express them. He was also willing to listen and grudgingly accepted that the Trail was a means by which many Australians as well as the occasional international traveller could learn to appreciate the bush. Today he is a self-appointed defender of the Trail (and fights the Authorities who dare ignore its needs). He welcomes genuine trekkers with a pot of tea and a few tales, and keeps a ready rifle to deter unwelcome hoons. He reckons he can tell which is which by the state of their Driza-Bones and Akubras.

To pass his muster your coat needs to look as though it may have been slept in on cold nights. If the front has been roughed up from shoeing the odd horse, or grimy from sheltering the odd new born beast, so much the better. A definite no-no is a coat whose rear vent is still firmly closed, or the fantail which has never been stretched over a saddle. Your hat needs to have character and a shape uniquely its own. Its history can be read from its shape, so it should not only have protected you from the sun but also given your head a long splash of water from the creek, or your horse a good drink from the spring.

Probably one of the most interesting characters you could meet along the Trail or anywhere in the bush is Herb Hain. Now in his mid seventies, with a large girth and awkward gait (the result of his last major accident with a horse) Herb's appearance belies the fact that he is one of the most respected and capable of the high country graziers.

The Hains in their Driza-Bones are as much a part of the landscape around the Snowy Mountains as the majestic snowgums. The Hain name is prominent throughout the history of Cooma where the family settled in 1854. Herb's grandfather and father were astute businessmen, building hotels and stores and developing some of the finest sheep country in the Monaro district. With such a background Herb's child-hood was comfortable, a Scots College education was supplemented by the then mandatory tour of the Old Country and The Continent. Herb soon discovered, however, that his heart lay in the high country and returned to make his life there.

Hain's Hut, which was built by Herb in 1947, is one of the better huts remaining from that era and still provides bushwalkers with a refuge from the elements.

He got to use the hut one day himself quite unexpectedly.

Herb liked to go out for weeks at a time with his good friend and fellow mountain legend, Tom Taylor. The two would explore every accessible inch of the high country, sometimes to track sheep, at other times just for the sheer joy of being there.

On this particular occasion they were doing a bit of fly fishing, from horseback. Herb was poking along the creek bank, casting in likely places when, without warning, his horse suddenly bucked, throwing him clear into the creek. The horse took off up the hill dragging the fishing line with it. When Tom finished laughing and Herb was fished out of the creek, the two made their way to Hain's Hut to spend the night and let Herb dry his clothes and regain some warmth.

The horse was finally tracked down some considerable distance from the hut next day. They found the fly firmly embedded in its genitals, where it remained for many months much to the discomfort of any observer but, luckily, less so for the unfortunate animal.

Herb Hain's love of the adventurous life in the Snowy Mountains led to his claim that he was the first person ever to go tobogganing there.

Each winter he would take the pack horses up into the mountains loaded with salt blocks to supplement the feed for the stock which grazed on the small grassy pockets left on the sheltered side of the mountain. He then had to get the blocks down to the places where the stock were sheltering and sometimes this meant going through fairly deep snow, manageable on skis but difficult with bulky blocks of salt to carry. Herb discovered that he could lay his Driza-Bone down flat on the snow, place two blocks of salt on it, then by sitting on the blocks and hanging on to the ends of the sleeves, he could ride his Driza-Bone to the bottom of the slope.

Driza-Bones are still worn by some skiers on the snowfields today and since the days of Herb's youth many a novice skier has inadvertently discovered the delights of tobogganing in a Driza-Bone after falling from his skis on the slopes.

THE STOCKMAN'S HALL OF FAME AND OUTBACK HERITAGE CENTRE

Another initiative which aims to preserve our outback heritage is the Australian Stockman's Hall of Fame and Outback Heritage Centre, sponsored in a small way by Driza-Bone. Located in Longreach, in central Queensland, at the junction of several stockroutes, this museum is the realisation of a dream for outback artist Hugh Sawrey. It was he who in 1974 envisioned a memorial to the people who carved out their living in the harsh and primitive conditions of the outback.

The design of the building was the result of a national competition, won in 1980 by Sydney architect Feiko Bouman. Combining sweeping iron roofs and vibrant outback colours it is host to a constant stream of visitors.

The Stockman's Hall of Fame and Outback Heritage Centre.

Fundraising, combined with support from the Commonwealth and Queensland governments, saw construction finally begin and the first building was completed in 1982. With the approach of the Australian Bicentenary, additional government funding became available. Construction then began in earnest and the buildings were finally completed in 1987.

After years of effort, the dream had been realised. On 29th April, 1988, 15,000 people from around Australia watched as Queen Elizabeth II opened the newly completed Stockman's Hall of Fame and Outback Heritage Centre.

A number of annual events held at the Stockman's Hall of Fame celebrate different aspects of Australia's outback heritage. The National Outback Performing Arts gathers performers to share in traditional outback entertainment including music and singing, poetry, recitation and yarn telling; while the Dame Mary Durack Crafts Awards encourage and preserve traditional outback crafts. These last are named in honour of the current director of the Hall of Fame, Dame Mary Durack-Miller, a noted Australian author and historian.

Eagle Street, Longreach in 1899

The Ringer's Muster, another annual event, reunites not only stockmen and drovers but also station managers, cooks, bookkeepers, storekeepers and governesses over a weekend of entertainment.

As well as its role as a place of reunion and celebration, the Stockman's Hall of Fame and Outback Heritage Centre is a living, growing museum and, as its full name suggests, is dedicated to preserving a record of times past. An oral history programme run by the Hall of Fame lists 400 people whose lives will eventually be recorded. This invaluable programme serves as a treasury of old-timers' stories, thus preserving the heritage of the outback.

Another programme which will keep the memory of outback heroes alive is the Unsung Heroes Register. This Register gives people the opportunity to record the stories of country people's lives, noting their contribution to outback life and lore.

Driza-Bone's sponsorship of the Stockman's Hall of Fame "Cowboy Poets" tour in March 1992 was inspired in part by a poem about Driza-Bone, written by Mark Gliori (which is reproduced on the next pages). The tour by American poets was a return visit after a group of Australian bush poets, nominated by the Hall of Fame, visited the USA in 1990. The group of American cowboy poets were selected by the Western Folklife Centre in Salt Lake City, Utah.

THE DRIZA-BONE LEGEND

He's camped in the middle of nowhere
The night is suffering cold
The stars are sharp and the dingo's eyes
Stare aghast from the big black hole
Home comforts are somewhat forgotten
As he boils the billy alone
Then he rolls out his swag by the fireside
                    And curls up in his Driza-Bone

Behind in the dark are the mountains
Climbing high to snow covered peaks
Where as a young man he had galloped
Through rich alpine forests and creeks
And now though his old bones are grating
He has answered the call of home
Returning the way he had left it
                    All wrapped up in his Driza-Bone

He dreams of the trails he has travelled
While combing the outback for work
Of droving with death on his doorstep
From the Kimberley through to Bourke
Of fighting the busters and duststorms
And heartbreaking rains on his own
But always secure in the knowledge
                    He was wrapped in his Driza-Bone

On the backs of rusty old rattlers
Or pushing along with the team
From cattle yards up at the 'Curry
To Flemington races he's been —
With love he has shared with the ladies
But his heart they'd only have known
To be true — when taken to fittings
                    For their very own Driza-Bone

But now he is back where he started
When snowflakes start falling around
When the crack of the whips are sounding
And cattle are keen to come down
So tomorrow he'll join his old mates
They'll all saddle up for old times
And with tattered old 'oilers' flying
                    They'll ride with the best of their kind

And should he make one final muster
When angels come calling his name
Forget the suits and razzamatazz
For he won't be there to complain
You can lay him down where you fancy
But his ghost will grumble and groan
Should you fail to grant his one last wish —
                    To be wrapped in his Driza-Bone

Mark Gliori

LEGENDS, LORE & LIES

TALL TALES OR TRUE?

Over the years the Driza-Bone grew to become as much a part of the squatters' and settlers' lives as a good horse or a yarn with friends. It was woven into the lore of the bush and tall tales told around twilight campfires. Whether the stories they told were true or whether they were told for amusement or as feats of exaggeration is of little consequence. But over time and telling, the Driza-Bone became as much a part of the legends as the heroes and the villains who were their owners. There were always stories about the wild bull (or feral pig, or cut snake) distracted by the flourish of a Driza-Bone. Or tales about the storm that was wilder than a shot pig, and the young lambs which insisted on coming into the world in the midst of it all and then had to be carried home in the safety of a Driza-Bone

It was also a part of everyday family life — which country kid hasn't crept outside in Dad's big, warm 'Driza' to do the chores whatever the weather, while his father searched the house in vain for the last place he left the darn thing.

Amazingly for what was traditionally a rural coat, the Driza-Bone has even become part of an urban myth which seems to surface each year

OPPOSITE PAGE
An entry in the 'Show us your Driza-Bone' competition captioned "Expose yourself to Poll Herefords."

around Royal Agricultural Show time. It is a time when country comes to town and the friendly rivalry between the bush dwellers and their city counterparts becomes a test of one upmanship

Even the weather joins in the fray, with Royal Show time being notorious for downpours of rain upon country visitors (who have been desperate for rain at home) and the city throngs (who dread the thought of splashing around the Show with wet ankles and whining kids). This weather brings out the Driza-Bones in force, and saddlery outlets in residence at the Show have been known to equal their total year's sales in just one week at a wet Show.

A Horse of a Different Coat

The urban myth (sworn by its tellers each year to have happened to someone they know well) tells of a bush visitor, complete with faithful old Driza-Bone, Akubra hat, R.M.Williams boots and moleskins wandering out of the rain and into the large pavilion housing the big Clydesdale horses in their stalls. As he stands there looking at these gentle giants, a well dressed city gent comes up and stands beside him, and looking in the same direction says to him, "I think these Drizedales are magnificent".

"Drizedales?" replies the bushie, and realising the townie's mistake and seeking, for the fun of it, to add to the confusion, "You mean Driza-Bones, don't you?"

"Yes of course, my mistake." replies the townie "My grandfather used to breed them" he boasts.

"I would have thought that impossible."

"No," he wisely assures the bushie in all sincerity, "not impossible but very difficult."

"Well then" says the bushie "I shall borrow my mate's coat to put over my old faithful and hope for twins so we can both get a new one."

The townie pauses a moment longer, smiles and walks away bemused, wondering about the confused farmer in the raincoat and his grasp on the facts of life.

*I'm an old and dusty
  Driza
Home for nought but
  redback spider
And the visits of a lonely
  slug or snail.*

THE TWO PROSPECTORS

Whether urban myths or bushie's legends, it is strange how the same stories are retold time and again, with small changes in detail depending on whether the tale is being recounted in cattle territory or sheep country, or where the gold mines and the prospectors once flourished. One such tale tells the story of two old prospectors who took refuge in a cattlemen's hut one night.

They had been away from civilisation for so many weeks that their supplies had long run out and they had been living on bush tucker and the occasional 'stray' sheep. The season was beginning to turn and the days were increasingly grey and rainy so they had decided to head back to town to exchange their meagre finds for more supplies and perhaps the odd job closer to town.

Earlier in the day along the stock route while heading for a cattlemen's hut known locally as the Mount Stirling Hilton, they had met a solitary stockman travelling in the opposite direction. He had traded them some Overproof Bundy for a couple of specks of gold and they had continued on their separate ways. By late afternoon they had reached the sanctuary of the hut. It was one of those squared log huts, with a straight stone fireplace and chimney across one end, and patched here, there and everywhere with corrugated iron. The Hilton it was not.

This refuge had been used by cattlemen and prospectors since time immemorial, and more recently by the new breed of bushwalkers who proclaimed respect for the bush but conveniently forgot to extend this to the huts left unlocked and stocked for their safety. The ground around the hut bore evidence of abandoned diggings by earlier prospectors now long gone. The inside of the hut bore evidence of more recent inhabitants with every removable piece of timber used for firewood. Gone were the kitchen cupboards, the drawers, even the odd floorboard. But to the two prospectors it held the luxury of shelter and beds.

They soon lit a fire from the kindling and dead timber which littered the area surrounding the hut, pulled off their hats and boots and then revelled in the comfort of the narrow, iron-posted bunks with their mattresses hollowed from the toll of years of sleeping bodies. They kept their Driza-Bones on against the draughts of the hut, and thoughts of food and cooking quickly gave way to the warmth of a few Bundys.

Some hours later when the fire had reduced to a few warm ashes the older prospector was woken by a yelling, grunting and thumping from outside the hut. It appeared the younger prospector, somewhat the worse for rum had fumbled his way into the fireplace for greater warmth. When he awoke he was staring up at a starry sky from the bottom of a deep shaft and, thinking he had fallen down an old mine, had struggled up the inside of the chimney to get out. Reaching the top, and thinking he had made it to safety, he turned to get his bearings in the blackness and took a step into the night. His mate, hearing the commotion, rushed outside expecting to see the other hurt on the ground, but there he was suspended from the corner of the chimney by the tail of his Driza-Bone, beating with his hands on the side of the hut.

Put Your Feet in the Pockets Mickey

There is another side to the Australian character that is not marked by tall tales and exaggerated feats, an unsung, unassuming side that quietly shows a great capacity for caring about mates and family.

Ernie Leggett was such a person. A butcher by trade, he ran a small butcher's shop in Cessnock in the late 1950s. To his customers he was a jovial soul, in the way that butchers often are, always with time to take an interest in the activities of his customers, the comings and goings of their children and the state of the weather.

Ernie came from a long line of butchers and beneath the jolly demeanour was a hard worker and a hard taskmaster. He was an honest toiler for he also owned and operated his own small abattoir and worked long hours in buying, agisting, killing and preparing the meat before his shopkeeper's day had even begun. His father and brother both worked as fellow butchers in the shop while grandmother and aunt shared counter duties and bookkeeping responsibilities. Even the grandchildren were expected to do their bit in the holding yards at the abattoirs, and at the home property mustering the agistment stock.

Chris Leggett, Ernie's grandson, recalls him in his own words. "My memory of my grandfather has over the years begun to fade but there are a few characteristics that as a child were imprinted into my brain as indelible memories of him.

He was a very big man. He always smoked a pipe and had the sweet aroma of tobacco. He always carried a cane cattle prodder with a large leather flap at one end and a plaited leather handle at the other. He always wore, or had in the car, a large dark coloured coat with a funny smell.

My most vivid memory of him is when I was an overweight, uncoordinated 10 year old desperately striving to take my place in a family whose livelihood depended upon cattle, sheep, pigs and the working horses. My older brothers had been pulling their weight around the property for some years and now it was my turn. However, two small problems prevented me from helping the family I was otherwise so much a part of.

First, I could not ride a horse, and second, I was terrified of horses.

My father had tried in vain to bridge the gap between myself and the horse. My mother, perhaps through the transference of my own fears, lived in dread of my being injured, and my cousins and brothers all gave me a very hard time.

It was at this point that my grandfather Ernie Leggett, stepped in.

Des Castine introduces his son D.J. to horse riding in the safety of Dad's Driza-Bone coat.

One Sunday afternoon, Papa, as we called him, came to our house and insisted that I go with him to the abattoirs to help him with a small job. Filled with importance at having been singled out I drove with him in the old Chevvy to the near-deserted abattoirs. Leaving the car, we walked down to the bottom paddock and while I stood at a discreet distance he caught Piebald, the old mare that had always been his mount during my lifetime.

Curiosity was getting the better of me, yet I hesitated to ask what we were going to do in the hope that by keeping quiet I could avoid involvement in anything equine.

"What are we going to do Papa?" I finally ventured with some foreboding.

"Well, Mickey, we're going for a ride" (Mickey was what everyone in the family called me, perhaps somewhat aptly, after my hero Mickey Mouse.)

"But I can't ride Papa!" I cried, feeling trapped.

"Leave it to me Mickey, you'll be right".

I was unconvinced, but he was my grandfather and although I loved him dearly he was not someone you would readily argue with.

Papa saddled the fat old mare and then did the strangest thing. He took his Driza-Bone coat, unrolled it and threw it over the saddle. He then carefully arranged the coat so that the pockets fell behind and to each side of the saddle. Mounting the mare, he called me to his side and in one motion pulled me up behind him.

"Put your feet in the pockets, Mickey and hang on to me, you'll be right as rain".

Those pockets were deep and welcomingly secure. I clung to Papa's back for dear life for the best part of an hour before the steady roll of Piebald's walk and Papa's reassuring conversation began to ease the tension in my fingers and legs, and unbent my back enough so that with a new found cockiness I could survey the world from my new perch.

Papa was wise enough not to rush my new found confidence and in the weeks that followed we progressed to a bumpy trot and then to a wonderful rocking-chair canter before letting me ride solo on Piebald.

From that day my confidence grew, I learnt to ride, I mustered cattle, joined the local pony club, and even began to travel the local show circuit to test my campdrafting skills. None of this would have happened if it had not been for a Driza-Bone coat and a wonderul man who cared enough to understand and who took time for an overweight and fearful ten year old.

THE EMU EGGS

Part of the dry Australian humour is in the telling of stories against oneself. Dick Medcalf from out Cowra way in NSW tells the story of the time he felt he lost a part of himself, "You know a leg, or maybe a big strip of hide off me back; and I guess that's about what the old Driza-Bone was after all them years. The old coat sort of grew on me, I'd had her so long. Bought her about 36 or 37 years ago I'd say about the time of the 1950s floods out on the 'Bidgee between Narrandera and Hay, and she was sort of christened in them floods.

Red mud, flyblown sheep, horse sweat, cow yards, well you know what cow yards are. They all added their bit of, er, character to the old coat.

Then we had to re-build miles of fence. That barbwire near broke me heart, and what it did to the old coat! But she held out, some of them press studs tore, but bits of tie-wire, a length of bale twine, and a bit of emery glue worked wonders. She sort of matured, you might say.

So instead of keepin' her for special occasions like cattle sales or sheep sales and Sunday church, she sort of grew on me, a part of me if you like, and I wore her most of the time, rain hail or shine.

Course, I used her to cover all sorts of things. Take the pigs now, as sure as eggs, come a thunder storm or a howlin' gale in winter, the old sows are sure to start havin' suckers! Not, I might tell yer, under the good old half tank stand in the yard — no — out in the middle of the cow paddick! Well, you can't let new born piglets get wet and cold so I had ter wrap them in somethin' didn't I? Yes, the old Driza-Bone, only natural, she keeps out a gale don't she?

Then comes lamb markin'. This is the final happenin', the trajerdy I calls it.

We musters the mallet paddick when the kids finds three emu eggs, foxes had rolled them out of the nest, and they must 'ave been out in the weather since last winter, all through the heat and cold. So I says to the kids 'handle them eggs careful like and put 'em down somewhere safe'.

We'd done half the mob, about 500 lambs, me wearing me old Driza-Bone, she'd got a bit coated with blood and stuff, usual with lamb markin, and we starts again... or means to.

Old George and the kids says 'Dad, get on the other side of the yard that old coat pongs'. Well the wind's blowin in their faces so, bein' obliging, I steps over the fence.

Well, I did me stint in New Guinea in the War, hit the dirt when the Japanese started shelling, crawled inter the mud when the mortars cracked BUT, when I stepped over that fence I reckonned I'd hit the best land mine ever. She really rocked me and everyone else includin' the sheep. So, I hits the dirt! You guessed it, right on top of them emu eggs! Talk about explosive! And STINK!

The old Driza-Bone, well, she'd taken most of it, the coat was even more khaki maybe yeller and green in streaks runnin all over. She was tattered and torn near up ter me belt, and then old George starts, 'Get ter hell outa here yer old stinkin so and so, head fer the dam. Don't come near!' Positive rude he was, so I heads fer the dam and peeled off. Tried ter sluice the old Driza-Bone down in the water but a sort of green scum floats all across the dam and I had ter scrub meself with mud, boy did that stuff stink and stick!

Anyway, the kids and old George cut three holes in a couple of chaff bags and I pulls them on. Me pants was rooined, me boots was full of greasy muck, and I reaches for me Driza-Bone.

'Not on her life' yells George and grabs a long piece of No. 8 wire and, standin' well back, hooks the old coat over to the fire we'd lit to burn the lambs tails.

Then I tells yer true… the old so and so throws me old Driza onter that there fire. Well I stands there and watches her die. She sorts of spat and hissed a bit, pretty soon only the press studs was left glowin' in the ashes. I feels me heart kick, fair dinkum, ter see me old mate die!

That's about the end. I'm still eatin' on the back verandah, right where me old coat 'uster hang, Mum and the kids eats in the dinin' room, reckons them emu eggs is still clingin' a bit…"

300 Miles North West of The Alice

One characteristic that binds Australians together is their ability to remember unique experiences when gathered around a keg of beer or a campfire. There's always a bigger story to be told, and Mick Neill at Salt Creek in South Australia has never been one to be outdone.

"There I was, three hundred miles north west of the Alice, perched on the top rail of the portable cattle yards, and the only things keeping out the icy July winds and drizzle were my old Driza-Bone and Akubra. I was looking over a mob of scrubbers the choppers had just driven in, thinking what bastards they would be to load, when out of the middle of them burst the biggest, meanest looking scrub bull I have ever seen! He had two pick handles for horns and a neck like an elephant and was heading straight for the panel I was sitting on. He drops his head and hooks those bloody great horns under the bottom rail and, with a mighty bellow, lifts the side of the yard and starts to go out underneath.

I quickly hooked my legs through the rails and, whipping off the old oilskin as the big bugger passed beneath me, I flung it over his head blinding him. Well he careered across the flat in a mad panic and crashed straight into the cook's caravan knocking it arse up. Out comes the cook screaming blue murder and causing the bull to run like hell from the noise straight into the road train which goes over on its side like a toy truck. The big bugger staggered a bit, then regained his footing and thundered off toward the scrub. I was sure now that we'd lost him but then the clumsy great bugger trod on the dangling coat sleeve in full stride and with an earth shuddering crash he hit the ground! I flew over there as quick as I could and sure enough the mighty beast had broken his neck. What a state of affairs! An $800 bull dead, the cook's caravan destroyed and the road train stuffed!

I pulled my Driza-Bone back on and it was still in one piece which was lucky. After all a bloke was starting to get cold without it."

The Store on Commonwealth Hill

Peter Mudge from the Mouth of the Murray, down Goolwa way, likes to remember a particular day, "We were cleaning out the store on Commonwealth Hill which was the biggest sheep station in the world as we'd proudly tell any townies or tourists who'd listen. It was a hundred miles long by forty five miles wide and I'd gone up as overseer, straight from the South East of South Australia, where one square mile was considered a big spread.

The Manager was away on holidays and Eileen, the Pommie book-keeper, thought we should spruce the place up a bit. I shrugged off my grimy old Driza-Bone and kicked it behind the door of the store which supplied the station staff and their families. We started on the bottom shelves and gradually worked our way up. Petrified prunes, rusty cans of dog food, cornflake packets doing time as apartments for mice; out it all went. Three ute loads later the place was starting to look respectable.

The rubbish heap for the station was about 100 yards long and 100 years high. In the outback there is no convenient, twice weekly council rubbish removal so you do it all yourselves. You could trace the history of motoring in Australia just by walking around the heap. And we too had added to it in our own small way. There were T-Model Ford carcasses right up to late model Holdens which had been written off by crazy jackaroos.

I set fire to the rubbish, the standard procedure, rolled a smoke and sat on the tailgate of the ute watching the flames for a while before heading back to the homestead, about a mile away. I was nearly halfway when the saltbush suddenly lay flat to the ground and then stood up again. Seconds later, an almighty bang made me whip my head around and I stared in amazement at a sight I'll never forget. A hundred years of rubbish was suspended high in the air. Car bodies, rusty tanks, oil drums, motorbike frames were all just parked up there in the sky.

My knees were still knocking as I went up the store steps to see if Eileen could shed any light on what had just happened. I knew that even petrified prunes didn't have the explosive power that I'd just witnessed. She was sitting at her desk wiping the blood off her face where the window got her as it was shattered by the blast.

"What do you reckon happened?" I stuttered. She shook her head. "The only thing I chucked out that was a bit odd was a box of old brown candles from up in the rafters. I wrapped them up in an old raincoat because the box they were in fell to bits."

Yes, my Driza-Bone had gone to heaven with petrified prunes and cornflake packets for company.

The mystery remained for another week until the Manager returned from his holidays.

"A case of sweating gelignite" he told us. "I put it up there so no-one would trip over it. The detonators were in an old Cornflakes packet, but I see they've gone too. Pity about the Driza-Bone, would have still had a few good years in it."

The Year of the Big Wet

When it rains, a Driza-Bone is your best friend. But in a dry season it's probably about as well remembered as the name of the horse which came second in the Melbourne Cup last year.

Mrs Patrick recalls the last Big Wet out west. That was the year she bought her Driza-Bone. She hadn't needed one for a few years but in this particular year, the one they called the Big Wet, it rained

three times in a month, buckets of it, and in a place where it is usually so dry that if it rains more than twice in a month it's called a record wet season.

In this district the countryside is unused to downpours like these and because the land is so flat the water can't escape. That always means a flood.

"On one particular day," Mrs Patrick recollects "and I remember it well because I'd worn my Driza-Bone three days in a row (which is unheard of out here), my husband George and I went to check the sheep in the top paddock. Why we called it the top paddock I'll never know. It was

Sally Cripps from Blackall in Queensland calls this picture Mustering 1990 style.

the lowest bit of ground on the place, and being closest to the creek, it was always the first bit to flood.

Here I must make mention of George, that queer old bloke I married in a daze thirty-seven years ago. He was so set in his ways he still wore red flannel longjohns, which probably explains why he came to be wearing an old chaff bag over his head and shoulders instead of something as new fangled as a Driza-Bone in the Wet.

Well, George and I went out to check the sheep in the top paddock, me in my Driza-Bone (Thoroughly Modern Myrtle he called me) and him a sight with that old chaff bag sitting up on his head, like he belonged to some strange religious sect. Even his old dog growled at him.

It was raining something terrible. Old George was soon soaked but, under my coat, I was dry as a you know what. There was so much water about that even the dog went home. The sheep, poor beggars, were all crowded round the gate swimming for their lives in the water, weighed down by their wool and bleating to be let through.

So we waded in, water up to our knees, and George yells at me to open the gate so he can count the sheep as they go past. I had a huge struggle to open it because of the build up of mud. And then all of a sudden, when I finally yanked it open, the water from the other side of the gate rushes through in a big wash taking with it all the sheep, and of course, old George in their midst.

"Help!" yelled George at the top of his voice, floating away with the sheep, "Myrtle, help!"

I could have ignored him, but I didn't. "Hang on!" I yelled back, and without thinking, ripped off my Driza-Bone and flung it as far out as I could to old George. To this day I'm not sure why.

Well, he caught it, and he and about two hundred sheep tried to climb aboard. The last I saw of him and the mob, they were floating away in

Mr and Mrs P. Bannatyne
weather the elements to get the
job done.

the rain, clinging to my Driza-Bone. He might have floated on forever
but he finally got caught in the neighbour's deer fence and got help.

Nowadays, old Gorgeous George swears by his Driza-Bone. He leaves it
hanging close to hand by the back door, even in the year of the Big Dry,
right next to the longjohns… and the chaff bags for the sheep.

THE DOG FROM PLUVIAL HILL

Of course, in the parts of Australia where it rains more than it shines, the Driza-Bone tales become even taller.

When the pioneers established a township at Pluvial Hill it was really a triumph of optimism over expediency. Only the highway kept it alive. That and the fact that as the wettest hole in Australia it attracted a few curious tourists. Like most other small Australian towns, Pluvial Hill had its Paragon Cafe with pinball machines, dusty jars of oysters and pickled onions. Its Criterion Hotel with rotting verandah posts was much favoured by the town dogs for having the only dry posts in the district. And its motor garage still sported faded advertisements for Plume Motor Spirit and Vacuum Oil.

But what Pluvial Hill had mostly was rain. It rained, on average, about 300 days a year. The other 65 days were either hail or snow. This explains the curious fact, noted by passing tourist buses, that every inhabitant of the district wore a long brown coat, fastened high up on the neck and split up the back to the top of the legs. As Dan Herlihy, the octogenarian motor garage proprietor often pointed out, ordinary raincoats were "orright fer blokes goin' from one verandah t'other" but at Pluvial Hill you needed "some dacint protictshun".

This remarkable showing of waterproofs was the first thing that the stranger noticed when he pulled up at the Criterion. He was one of these macho city types desperately searching for a "bush image". His petrol guzzling four wheel drive was bedecked with jerry cans, trewhella jacks and roo bars. From the front hung an enormous anchor chain and the back window sported a variety of intelligent stickers such as "Fertilize the bush — doze in a greenie".

He had come in search of a dog. Well, not the dog really, but the coat that went with it. The advertisement had read "good working dog, 2 year old, plus Driza-Bone coat — $50 the lot". After certain enquiries at the pub and the usual bush directions he found himself at the doorway of McPherson's farmhouse.

"A canny dog" said McPherson, pointing to the kennel near the fowl pen. They walked across to the spot, dodging the puddles and a group of forlorn hens huddled by the wood heap. The stranger peered into the kennel and there, to his utter amazement, was a kelpie dog wearing a beautifully tailored Driza-Bone and leaning nonchalantly against the wall of his kennel.

"The missus altered the coat for him" explained McPherson. "Puts it on himself too" he added, "but he has a bit of trouble with the two top studs near the neck."

Mrs Pay and her pampered pooch complete with custom made Driza-Bone.

"Extraordinary" gasped the stranger.

"He can read too" said McPherson in quite a matter of fact tone. "Started with road signs but now the missus brings home books from the library".

"Be damned" said the stranger. "That can't be true".

McPherson looked hurt. "I'm not a bloody liar man, the dog can read . He's halfway through Gibbon's Decline and Fall of the Roman Empire". We got him something with a bit of bulk to keep him occupied 'til next market day".

"Good Lord man", exclaimed the Stranger. "Why would you want to sell a dog like that?"

McPherson shook his head sadly. "He's useless here", he said. "He's joined the union and the bugger won't work in the rain."

THE GHOST IN THE BROWN DRIZA-BONE

English castles have their ghosts, Scotland its watery monster, America its haunted houses, but Australia can lay claim to a ghost of a different colour. A ghost in a brown Driza-Bone.

Legend has it that a group of stockmen were sitting around a campfire one night after their meal. The night was still before an approaching storm. The talk had died down, and with the warmth of the fire, a long day's work and the drowsy effects of a campfire meal they were beginning to comfortably doze off. A big male possum, attracted by the food scraps and emboldened by the night ventured close to the fire.

His activities soon woke one of the stockmen who, without thinking, picked up the Driza-Bone lying next to him and threw it at the animal.

With an accuracy the stockmen later regretted, the coat landed on top of the possum and, blinded, it took off with the Driza-Bone over its head. In an effort to rid himself of the coat the possum reared onto its hind legs as it ran, and with its arms tried to divest himself of this obstruction. However all this action managed to achieve was that the possum's arms slid into the upper reaches of the sleeves.

The ensuing commotion quickly awoke the others who, not having seen what happened, saw only a very small, darkly clad figure running away from them in a Driza-Bone coat and waving his arms.

The possum, panic struck and unseeing ran straight into the mob of cattle, scattering them in contagious panic in every direction. It tried to scramble up the nearest tree, but as luck would have it chose a hefty bull's hind leg, clawing its way up onto the bull's back. The bull, snorting and bucking went berserk and tore through the herd, stampeding them. In no time the pounding herd had cleared a track a mile wide, in their terror smashing everything in their path.

The stockmen, now mounted, rode off in hot pursuit into the pitch darkness.

They finally managed to steady the herd, to slow it and finally to wheel it in a clearing; but the cattle, who were still restless, could not be calmed sufficiently before the storm broke and tired stockmen and spent horses rode the herd on through the night and throughout the storm.

That bull was never seen in the herd again, but stockmen ever since have reported sighting him on nights before a storm, still with a small Driza-Bone clad rider clinging to his back, and have been able to accurately forecast the start of the Big Wet by his appearance.

THE ORIGIN OF THE BUNYIP

Of course no recounting of Australian ghost stories would be complete without some reference to the Bunyip, a (some say) mythical creature which had its roots in Aboriginal lore. The Bunyip is said to inhabit waterholes, billabongs, swamps and river bends, and reportedly has a rather special taste for women.

Various sightings have recorded the Bunyip as having fur, feathers, fishy scales and/or a shiny brown coat. It has a long tail or an elongated neck (depending on which end you thought you saw). Half man, half animal, it is tall with a round head, big eyes, long ears and utters a blood curdling cry when approached.

Sightings of the Bunyip were at their height during the years of the Great Depression but as the twentieth century draws to a close they have become less and less frequent. Could it be that the myth of the Bunyip is waning, or perhaps it is encroaching civilisation which is threatening it with extinction.

I therefore hesitate to dispel the myth of the Bunyip but perhaps its true origins should be recorded before it disappears from our midst altogether.

During the Great Depression and, to a lesser extent at other times, itinerant workers, swaggies and those wishing to escape the long arm of the law, or the arms of wives and children, rolled a few belongings in a swag and took to the road.

They travelled the byways and the backblocks, and those with a preference for solitude and the ability to live off the land often went bush and as far away from civilisation as their survival would allow. They came to know the remote natural springs and waterholes essential to their existence.

DRIZA-BONE SPECIAL FEATURES

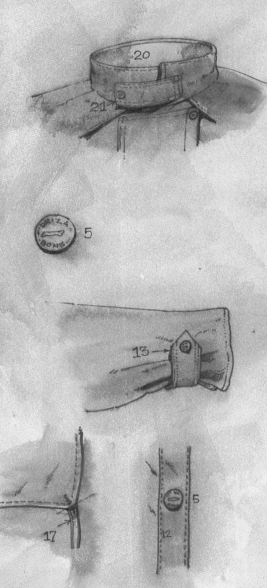

1   Generous width for shoulder movement.
2   Kitchen door hook hanger.
3   Free flowing cape.
4   Double snap closure.
5   Quality brass snaps.
6   Sleeve length to finish midway down hand.
7   100% cotton lining.
8   Inside poachers pockets for valuables.
9   Reinforced elbows.
10 Deep roomy weatherproof pockets.
11 Storm flap protects against head-on weather.
12 Waxed thread fills holes made by sewing.
13 Adjustable double wrist snaps to shorten sleeves and/or keep rain from running down arms.
14 Double fabric over shoulders prevents cold shoulder from body heat condensation.
15 Back flap closing snaps.
16 Saddle cover (fantail).
17 Arm straps to keep cape down.
18 Sturdy leg straps for windy conditions and to keep coat over legs and knees while riding.
19 Heavy duty double stitched.
20 Collar is cotton lined for comfort.
21 High neck strap snap closure.

PLAN FOR DRIZA-BONE

RIDING COAT
T. WEEKES.
No: 173947-ARC-3

Those who stayed near the major rivers camped in the cool of the river bends and became known as walers or whalers to the passengers on the passing paddle steamers of the big river systems.

The origin of the name whaler is obscure but one explanation is thought to lie in the swaggie's similarity in appearance to a beached whale when camped beneath his swag or old Driza-Bone. The other possibility is that they were first seen in New South Wales along the banks of the Murray and Murrumbidgee Rivers.

The more reclusive the swaggie, the more remote were the waterholes and billabongs he sought for survival. When he heard the very occasional approach of a horse and rider he would make for the cover of water and hide among the reeds with his Driza-Bone over his head to give himself a breathing space.

By doing this the swaggie hoped to remain unseen or at worst be taken for a piece of flotsam or jetsam. When he thought the coast was clear he would surface and if the luckless observer was still around he would no doubt have the living daylights scared out of him by the strange apparition rising out of the water.

Alas, the truth is told, the Bunyip is nothing but a reclusive swaggie wearing a Driza-Bone.

His appearance can be attributed to the state of his attire after months, if not years on the road, not to mention the clinging mud, leaves and weeds from his dunking in the billabong.

As to his blood curdling cry, well that was in fact the poor swaggie giving vent to his own fright on being sighted by an onlooker when he thought himself alone. His predilection for waterholes and billabongs was necessary to his own survival.

And his preference for scaring off, or alternatively, making his presence known to women was, well, understandable.

The Great Paddle Steamer Race

The paddle steamer captains of the Murray River were among the first as well as the most frequent to see the mythical Bunyip or the more common whalers along the river's banks. (One of the early paddle steamers was even given the name *Bunyip*.) These intrepid skippers created a few legends in their own right, and one such a tale involves the intense rivalry which existed between the paddle steamer captains and its culmination in a race down the great river.

The Murray River winds its way through 2600 kilometres of Australian countryside in a ribbon of giant loops, doubling back on itself time after time. It was navigable to the paddle steamers for eight months or so of the year, dependant upon the rains upstream to raise the river level after dry seasons. To be a successful skipper on the Murray meant an intimate knowledge of the river with its twisting and turning bends, its hazardous currents and ever changing sandbanks.

Crews were away for months at a time, or if they were unfortunate enough to be separated from their home base in times of drought they may have been away for a year or more if the river depth fell and the sandbanks blocked their route home. The record length of time away from home was three years because of drought, but it is told that the same boat made the return journey in two weeks down the fast flowing flood waters when the rains eventually came.

There was no local shipbuilding industry in the early days of the riverboats and many of the ships' boilers had been built for farmers or had been seconded from the railways. There were no conveniently located ships' chandlers or shipwrights to radio (not that they had radios) when the paddle steamers broke down or needed running repairs. So to be a successful skipper also meant having a canny ingenuity (or at least a plumber or carpenter on board). Collisions with sunken red gumtrees were not uncommon and at least one ingenious captain

was heard to quickly order a meal of lamb chops after his steamer was snagged by a fallen red gum. The fat from the chops was used very effectively to plug the leak.

The "Tarella" on a cruise down the Murray.

The arrival of the paddle steamer, heralded by a distant puff of smoke, was a welcome event for the squatters and settlers along the route of the Murray. The steamer brought mail, supplies, shearing teams and family visitors to these far flung settlements, and later picked up the wool bales for transport to Goolwa at the mouth of the river for shipping overseas.

The skippers with the most successful records and reputations for delivering the goods (and the visitors) on time were the most sought after. Their reputations for reliability were fiercely guarded and stories are bountiful about the rivalry between the paddle steamers and the lengths their captains went to in delivering their cargoes and passengers.

Even hundreds of kilometres inland the riverboats and their passengers faced being swamped in treacherous storms. On calm, sunny days they could still capsize if the captain cut the river bends too finely. They braved danger too in navigating the fallen timber along the swollen river banks in times of flood. And in times of drought there was the risk of being marooned far from their destinations, facing either the prospect of turning back to their previous port or having to offload their passengers to finish their precarious journey overland.

Yet in spite of the intense competition which existed between them, and the race to complete their journeys before the water level dropped, the one thing all the captains agreed upon was that Sunday would always be a day of rest. That was until the captain of the *Lady Hopetown* discovered a way around this gentlemen's agreement.

The Adelaide Company was trying to encourage wealthy settlers to come to the still new and struggling colony of South Australia. One incentive was the promise of a purse of some two thousand two hundred pounds to the captain of the paddle steamer which was first to deliver five passengers who, on arrival in South Australia, would purchase land in the colony at the going price of twelve shillings per acre.

Previous schemes at attracting wealthy squatters had failed miserably and the persuasive powers of the land based agents and the prized reputations of their river boat captains was a last ditch effort by the colony's failing masters. For the skippers too this was to be a final effort to ensure the success of the South Australian end of their business for the south western reaches and the mouth of the Murray River lay in that colony.

The *Lady Hopetown* was not among the first of the paddle steamers to set out in this quest, for she was further downstream than the others when the race was announced, so not only had she still to pick up her valuable passengers but she also had much water to make up on her sister ships.

The first steamer she was able to pass was the *Gauntlet*, rudely awakening her crew at midnight as she steamed past with lights ablaze. Curfew for the steamers was officially 10.30pm, but on nights with a good moon this was often ignored and Captain Blackall took full advantage of a strong set of reflector headlamps on the *Lady H.* and a guiding moon.

Then at first light she belched past another riverboat, the *Lady Adey*, in a bustle of black smoke, funnels aglow from the furious stoking of her boilers below.

Every skipper worth his salt marked his own maps of the river to show permanent snags, the location of sandbanks, the river depths at various times of the year, and the safe speeds around the tight bends for his particular vessel (the shorter the vessel the faster they could negotiate the bends). The most treacherous parts of the river are known even to this day by the names given to them by the paddle steamer skippers. The most dangerous bends are known as Cape Horn and the Devil's Elbow, and a stretch thick with snags which is still called Hell's Gate by the old timers. One particularly notorious reef and its rapids are referred to as the Bitch and Pups (though the name is usually shortened by despairing navigators).

You may even find Lady's Leap still marked on navigational maps, named after the intrepid *Lady Hopetown*, but more of that later.

Word had spread by the bush telegraph that Blackall and his crew were pushing hard, and this spurred on the skipper of the *Binnalong* who, in his haste and to his peril, broadsided on the Bends. Stuck fast and with night falling around him, he lit all the lanterns to warn off others and waited for the dawn. Captain and crew were up with the first light to pull her off the shore with ropes but in the night the currents had banked the sand firmly along her sides. At first light therefore those

The "Gem" moored on the Murray.

on board the *Lady H.* saw the *Binnalong* crew standing in the water shovelling desperately to dig her out as they swept by on the current.

The *Doubtless* was the next luckless steamer to line up in the *Hopetown's* sights and a duel of navigational skills ensued between the rival skippers, each hoping to trick the other into misjudging the width or clearance of a sandbar. The *Lady H.*, the smaller of the two vessels, passed the *Doubtless* on a curve but was overtaken on a straight stretch where power counted. The *Doubtless'* powerful boiler belched black smoke and embers rained with hisses upon the river as she steamed past. Instead of gathering more speed, mysteriously, the *Doubtless* began to slow, its boilers still furiously working up a full head of steam. The smirking crew of the *Lady H.* passed the *Doubtless* again and left her as though standing still in the wake. Minutes later an explosion was heard behind the *Lady H.* and crew and passengers looked on amazed as debris from the *Doubtless'* boiler and its decking rose high into the air.

Weeks later the salvage crews reported finding a long rope wrapped around the paddle wheel of the unfortunate *Doubtless*, but whether it had been dropped by a careless deckhand or tossed from the *Lady H.* has never been determined.

The *Lady Hopetown* passed two more steamers without much of a fight, and was now heading down the home stretch. Ahead lay the *Pride of Echuca* and *The Dew* (named because its shallow draught enabled it to continue sailing when the river dropped and it was said she could sail upon nothing but the morning dew). The *Pride* was the most powerful boat on the river and *The Dew* could navigate where no others could follow. The captains were brothers and it was rumoured they had agreed to combine their efforts to win the race and share the prize money.

They were formidable opposition, but the Captain of the *Lady H.*, an experienced ocean sailor as well as a master riverboat skipper matched them in know-how as well as dare-devilry.

First into the fray was the slower *Dew* which managed to keep the *Lady H.* at bay until a long straight stretch enabled the *Lady* to lift her skirts and run at full steam. On the next bends she caught sight of the *Pride* lumbering her great length around the curves. She began to gain on the *Pride*, but so too did *The Dew* who again passed the *Lady* in the bends. The stretch ahead was straight but treacherous, with sandbars forcing the riverboats into narrow channels. Again *The Dew* had the advantage with her shallow draught, and it is here that the *Lady* leapt into history, but whether by good seamanship or good fortune the history books have been reticent to judge.

The Dew was just ahead of the *Lady* in the channel when Captain Blackall cut to the inside, perhaps thinking he could force *The Dew* over, or perhaps he just misjudged the depth of the water over the sandbank. The *Lady* hit the sand at full steam, and such was her speed that her bow and front half became airborne, her paddlewheel churning through the sand and her momentum carrying her over the bar and ahead of *The Dew*. Today that point in the river is still recognised as the Lady's Leap.

She continued to gain considerable ground on the *Pride* but it had too much distance and cleared the bends before the *Lady* could draw level.

By Saturday nightfall both crews were exhausted and at such times the greatest danger is in small misjudgements. The *Lady H.* was the first to succumb when the leading hand was taking soundings of a dangerously narrow channel with a long pole. An unseen rock barred the *Lady*'s progress and the sailor was thrown overboard by the sudden jolt of the boat being thrown off course.

The holing was inconvenient but not serious and repairs could be effected within hours. The greater danger was yet to come however for the sudden detour had brought them perilously close to the river bank and the overhanging red gums bowed low over the river to seize intruders in their domain. The *Lady*'s superstructure was decapitated in one fell swoop, leaving her with funnel gone and no deckhouse. Her paddlewheel housing remained entangled in the overhang, and axes and saws were called for to loosen her from the red gum's grip.

Again she was passed by *The Dew*, the race now was as good as over for not only had she lost some vital parts in her decapitation but tomorrow was the Sabbath, a day laid down by the race organisers as one on which the boilers must not be stoked, for that was the devil's delight. By midnight *The Dew* and the *Pride of Echuca* were moored for the duration of the day of rest, with the safety of several hours' sailing time separating them from the crippled *Lady Hopetown*.

One long day's sailing distance from Goolwa, one day from victory. Crew and passengers on the *Lady H.* shared Captain Blackall's dismay as the crew worked through the following day to make her riverworthy in time for Monday. But there was little chance of catching the powerful

Pride, especially with *The Dew* running interference behind her to keep the *Lady* at a distance.

The race rules stipulated that both passengers and captain must finish the race and by dusk on Sunday evening Captain Blackall had convinced his passengers that there was a way, but they had to set sail immediately, albeit without boilers, for they needed the cover of night and twelve hours start in order to have any chance of succeeding.

As dusk began to lay its cover over the river, the crew lowered the *Lady*'s cargo of wool bales into the river and lashed several together. Poles were erected on the bobbing rafts and the crews' Driza-Bone coats were secured between the makeshift masts. The coats were buttoned one to the other and the sleeves slipped through the poles. The Driza-Bones had once been made from ships' sails and Captain Blackall saw no reason why they should not be put to their original task again. A steady breeze and a half moon helped them on their way.

Silently they slipped by *The Dew* and the *Pride of Echuca*, unseen by their crews or passengers, and with their shallow draughts sailed easily into the dawn. Along the river banks surprised settlers, on the lookout for the leading boats, heralded their arrival with gunfire salutes from their carbines, and when the makeshift boats bobbed into sight off Goolwa a small fleet of fishing vessels in turn hung their Driza-Bones from the masts to toast their ingenuity and welcome the victors.

To this day, if you see fishing boats near Goolwa with their nets hanging out to dry, you may also see an old Driza-Bone hoisted high in salute to the hardy paddle steamer captains who opened up the Murray and the settlement of South Australia.

Driza-Bone Maintenance

Caring For Your Coat

While the Driza-Bone museum attests to the durability of the product, there are a few hints which will help to keep your Driza-Bone in good condition. Remember, if you look after your Driza-Bone, it will look after you.

For a start keep your Driza-Bone away from spirits, acids and alkalis.

To remove mud from the coat leave it to dry first and then merely brush it off. It may be washed in warm water but don't use detergents or soap powders on them.

Keep your Driza-Bone well oiled and it will stay in good condition.

Remember, don't wear your coat around chemicals, oil or petrol.

Grease the studs if used near salt water and again, hose it down to keep it free of salt or grit.

The Driza-Bone coat is rot and mildew proofed but it helps if you don't roll it up or store the coat when it is still wet.

OPPOSITE PAGE
Turnout classes for the Australian Stock Horse Society specify Driza-Bone coats as part of the kit. This picture shows winner of the A.S.H. stallion class at the Sydney Royal Show, Glen Gough riding Yallatup Rivoli Rex.

How to Roll Your Own

One of the requirements in horse shows in the Australian Stock Horse Turnout Classes (classes that judge the appearance and presentation of horse and rider) is a Driza-Bone coat. The coat should be rolled up on the saddle if it is a nice sunny day, or should be worn if it is raining. If, on the other hand, the day starts out nice and pleasant but the heavens suddenly open up just as you pass the judge in your finely cleaned moleskins and pressed-to-perfection tweed jacket, then you will have points deducted for not being able to read the weather properly, even if the clouds have loomed threateningly for three months and nineteen days in a row without spilling a drop.

Unless you were born in the saddle and have been rolling your own Driza-Bone since the day they stopped pinning nappies on you, you may have thought that you were alone in the world in not being able to roll one into a reasonably neat and manageable bundle to tie to your saddle. (If the truth be known, Australian stockmen go to "Roll your own Driza-Bone" classes in kindergarten when their city cousins are discovering the joys of finger painting.)

Take heart, it has in fact been established beyond all reasonable doubt that the Driza-Bone has a life wish of its own when it is tied down, and can slither from the inside out to become longer and longer until it finally sheds itself of the baling twine or leather thongs which you thought were holding it in place. It will silently and stealthily go exploring under your horse's hooves unless you happen to ride looking down at the ground below you and recognise its intentions mid way through its travels.

Through some strange and unexplained quirk of nature the Driza-Bone is also able to grow corners and extra sleeves the minute you begin to roll it up. And the cape which sat so comfortably over your shoulders, when transferred to your saddle suddenly develops angles that catch on bushes which your horse instantly decides it likes to scrape past. They become handy pockets for dust and dying insects which would do an entomologist proud. Or in the event of your ever becoming terminally lost in the bush it will at least provide your rescuers with a complete record of your travels via the vegetation you have picked up en route. As a last resort you could also try eating the insects, twigs and torn leaves which accumulate in these corners and crevices, in which case you can then attribute your survival to your uncanny bush instincts and to being befriended by your amazing Driza-Bone.

However if you have no intention of becoming terminally lost in the bush you may like to know that there is, after all, a very simple way to roll your own Driza-Bone which not only creates the same neat bundle time after time, but also rolls away into a smaller bundle than you ever thought possible to fit onto your saddle, into your saddle bag, motorbike bag or even a briefcase.

Step 1   For a small neat roll, first take off your Driza-Bone.
Step 2   Snap close the press studs on the front of the coat.
Step 3   Then lay the coat flat, with the front facing upwards.
Step 4   Fold the sleeves into the centre, at a bit of an angle.
Step 5   Fold the two sides into the centre to form a long rectangle.
Step 6   Roll up tightly starting from the bottom of the coat.
Step 7   Then fold the cape around the roll so the inside of the cape covers the roll.

Voilà. And there you have the real reason for the cape on your Driza-Bone when it isn't raining.

A word of warning to the unwary. It is not recommended that you tightly roll up your Driza-Bone for any length of time when it is still wet. Apart from the fact that it may rain again any minute, you may find when you go to unroll it that it has not just a life of its own but has provided a nice moist breeding place for all sorts of little creatures indigenous to the Australian environment.

GLOSSARY

A GUIDE TO AUSTRALIAN SLANG

Akubra	the famed Australian-made felt hat, an essential part of country attire.
backblocks	the back section of a sheep or cattle station.
back of Bourke, beyond the black stump	any remote inland area a great distance from the speaker.
'Bidgee	Murrumbidgee River.
bloke	man.
blowie	blowfly.
blue	fight, mistake, nickname for redhead.
blue heeler	breed of Australian cattle dog.
bluey	swag or blanket roll carried by swagmen, drovers etc.
billy	a cylindrical metal container used for boiling water for tea.
billabong	an Aboriginal word for a waterhole that dries up or becomes isolated from its river in times of low rainfall.
brumby	a wild Australian horse.
bulldust	the deep, fine dust of the Outback roads.
bullocky	bullock dray driver.
bunyip	'mythical' creature known to inhabit billabongs and waterholes.
the bush	the untamed scrub, woods, forests of rural Australia in its natural state, also

refers to rural Australia in general.

bush tucker	food derived from the surrounding bush countryside (berries, roots, small animals etc).
bushed	tired, or lost (in the bush).
bushie	a person who lives in rural Australia.
Bundy	Bundaberg Rum.
camp oven	a cast iron container with lid used for campfire cooking, hot coals are placed over and around it. .
chooks	chickens.
cockatoo, cocky	white, crested parrot, aso a small scale farmer, particularly in Queensland.
cocky's joy	golden syrup.
cossies	swimming costumes/bathers/swimmers.
crook	dishonest person, no good, sick, bad, difficult ("feel crook", "crook weather", "crook job").
damper	bread made from flour and water, unleavened, usually cooked in a camp oven.
dingo	Australian native wild dog, tawny-yellow in colour.
dingo's breakfast	a yawn, a stretch and a look around.
dinkum	for real, true, honest, genuine.
dob in	inform on someone, contribute money, nominate someone for a task.
dog's breakfast	a mess.
dray	wagon or cart pulled by horses or bullocks.
Driza	Driza-Bone oilskin coat.
drongo	type of bird, fool.
the dry	the 7-8 months of the year in northern Australia when it doesn't rain.
duffers	cattle duffers, sheep duffers — cattle thieves, sheep thieves.
El Nino	a cyclical oceanic event which can have a significant influence on drought conditions in Australia. Its cycle tends southwards every 2 to 7 years.
fair dinkum	true, genuine.
galah	grey and pink parrot, foolish person.
jackaroo	station hand, usually trainee manager often the son of another landowner sent to work on other properties to learn different methods, soils, breeds etc.
jillaroo	female version of the jackaroo.

kelpie	breed of Australian sheepdog.
Kiwis	New Zealanders.
the long paddock	the grassed verge alongside roads and stockroutes, used for grazing in times of drought.
mate	good friend, used more casually in conversation to refer to an associate.
moleskins	cotton trousers designed for comfort and minimal abrasion in the saddle, they have a brushed finish echoing the softness of mole's fur.
Never-never	remote, isolated region of the outback.
O.P.	overproof (as in O.P. Bundy)
outback	remote, sparsely populated area of inland Australia.
paddock	field, pasture or fenced range.
pastoralist	owner of a large property used for grazing and crops.
R.M.s	R.M. Williams brand elastic sided boots.
scrub	an area covered in bush, trees, shrubs.
scrubbers	cattle mustered from the scrub which are unused to man and mustering.
shank's pony	on foot.
squatter	originally farmers who settled on Crown land, now refers usually to sheep station owners.
station	farm, ranch. Usually large sheep or cattle properties.
stockman	person employed to tend livestock.
stroppy	difficult, complaining.
swagman, swaggie	a man who travels the country on foot, and carries his belongings in a swag or bluey.
tin scratcher	a small time prospector.
top end	the northern end of the Northern Territory of Australia.
underground mutton	rabbit.
ute	utility motor car built like a small open backed truck and treated accordingly.
the wet	the rainy season, particularly the monsoonal or sub-monsoonal rains in northern Australia (December to March).

AUSTRALIAN SAYINGS

AGGRESSIVE	As a bull ant
ALIKE	As two peas in a pod
ANGRY	Madder than a cut snake
	To do your lolly (get angry)
	To do your block (get angry)
ASTONISHED	Like a stunned mullet
BLACK	As a burnt log
	As the inside of a cow
BUSY	Buzzing around like a blowfly
	Flat out like a lizard drinking
	Doing a fair swag
CLUMSY	As a duck in a ploughed paddock
COLD	As charity
	As yesterday's mashed potato
	As a mother-in-law's kiss
CONFUSION	Didn't know if he was Arthur or Martha
	Running around like a headless chook
	As clear as the moon on a foggy night

	As clear as mud
COURAGEOUS	As game as Ned Kelly
CRAZY	Has a kangaroo loose in the top paddock
CROOKED	As a dog's hind leg
DENSE COUNTRY	Too thick for a black snake to wriggle through
	Scrub so thick a dog couldn't bark in it (Banjo Paterson)
DEPART IN HASTE	Shoot through like a Bondi tram
DISHONEST	Lying like a mat on the floor
DISLIKE	I wouldn't piss in his ear if his brain was on fire
DISTANCE PLACES	The Black Stump
	Woop Woop
	Back of Bourke
	Where the crows fly backwards
EXPENSIVE	Charges like a Territory buffalo
TO BE FAIR	Fair crack of the whip mate
FLASHY	As flash as a rat with a gold tooth
FOOD	Cooking that would kill a brown dog
	Had a dingo's breakfast — a yawn, a stretch and a look around
FULL (or DRUNK)	As a goog (egg)
	As a tick
	As the last tram
	As a boot
	As a State school
HAPPY	As a dog with two tails
HEALTHY	Fit as a Mallee Bull
HEAT	Hotter than hell with the lid on
INHOSPITALITY	This must be where Burke & Wills (explorers) perished
HUMOROUS	That would silence a Kookaburra
	He's got more kid than a pregnant goat
HUNGRY	I'm so hungry I could eat a horse and chase the rider
INCREDULITY	Don't come the raw prawn with me
	What do you think this is — bushweek?

INTELLIGENT	No flies on him
	He didn't come down in the last shower
	Smarter than a swaggie with new boots on
MEAN	He's got deep pockets and short arms
	He wouldn't shout if a shark bit him
MISUNDERSTAND	Get hold of the wrong end of the stick
OBVIOUS	Blind Freddy could see it
OKAY	She's apples (apples and spice — nice)
	She'll be right
PLAIN	He's as plain as a back fence
SLOW	As a month of Sundays
	Dragging the chain
	As a wet week
SICK	Crook as Rookwood (famous Sydney cemetery)
STUPID	As a gumtree full of galahs
	A brick short of a load
	A sandwich short of a picnic
	Not the full quid
	Silly as a koala and not half as good looking
TALL	As long as a yard of pump water
THIN	Close one eye and you'd think he was a needle
	As thin as a match with the wood shaved off
UNCOUTH	Rough as guts
	Rough as old boots
UNDERHAND	Lower than a snake's belly
UNLUCKY	You've got Buckley's (none — Buckley's & Nunn was a famous store)
	If it were raining pea-soup he'd only have a fork
USELESS	As a wooden leg in a bushfire
	As a screen door on a submarine
	As a hole in a waterbag
WINDY	So windy it'd blow a dog off its chain
WILD	A horse so frisky it bucked its brand off

ACKNOWLEDGEMENTS

The author would like to thank the following people:
John L. Ferrif for *A Horse of a Different Coat*
R.H. Cleland for *The Two Prospectors*
Chris Leggett for *Put Your Feet in the Pockets Mickey*
Dick Medcalf for *The Emu Eggs*
Mick Neill for *300 miles North West of the Alice*
Peter Mudge for *The Store on Commonwealth Hill*
Jan Patrick for *The Year of the Big Wet*
B.J. 'Trapper' Coman for *The Dog from Pluvial Hill*
Saara Fitzsimons' poem *I'm an old and dusty Driza*
Mike Allen for Bicentennial National Trail stories
Driza-Bone Pty Ltd for access to their archives, photographs and patience
The Pickup Family
R.M. Williams
Natasha Rodgers
Simon Blackall

BIBLIOGRAPHY

New Zealand Patent Office
Brands An International Review by Interbrand. Golden Arrow Publications Ltd
Peter Phillips. *River Boat Days on the Murray, Darling, Murrumbidgee.* Lansdowne Press. 1972
Peter J. Phillips. *Redgum & Paddlewheels. Australia's Inland River Trade.* Greenhouse Publications Pty Ltd. 1980
R.M. Williams with Olaf Ruhen. *Beneath Whose Hand, the autobiography of R.M. Williams.* Pan Macmillan

Driza-Bone archives
Affidavit: R.E. Pickup

PICTURE ACKNOWLEDGEMENTS

The Watermark Press would like to thank all those who provided photographs and illustrations for this book. We would especially like to thank Anthony Browell for his cover photographs; Robert Lovell for his painting "In the Wet"; Chris Gladwell from the Australian Stockman's Hall of Fame (ASHOF) and Barbara Horten from David Jones for their assistance.

Every effort has been made to contact the copyright owners of the works included in this book. Where this has not been possible, please contact the publishers to ensure acknowledgement in future editions.

Specific credits with page numbers appear below.

12 *The Land* newspaper; 14 ASHOF; 15 ASHOF; 16 The Australasian Sketcher; 17 Robert Lovell *In the Wet*; 18 David Coventry; 20 Cyril Hume Collection; 22 Sydney Maritime Museum; 24 Sydney Maritime Museum; 26 *The Land* newspaper; 28 Ray Pickup; 29 Ray Pickup; 30 Simon Blackall; 32 Patent Trade Mark and Design Sub Office; 35 David Coventry; 36 Colleen Coles 38 David Jones archives; 41 David Seeto; 42 Tim Sharkey; 45 David Seeto; 47 Advertiser Newspapers; 50 ASHOF; 52 Tony McLeod; 53 Anthony Browell; 54 David Coventry; 59 Charlie Winter; 60 ASHOF; 61 David Jones archives; 62 Peter Rae/SMH; 64 Dalgety-N.Z.L. Merchandise Service Guide; 67 Alan Moir; 71 AAP Photo Library; 72 Victorian Tourist Commission; 74 Bicentennial National Trail; 77 Bicentennial National Trail; 82 ASHOF; 85 ASHOF; 86 ASHOF; 89 David Coventry; 90 David Coventry; 92 Australian Poll Hereford Society; 95 *The Land* newspaper; 99 Des Castine; 107 Anthony Browell; 108 Anthony Browell; 109 Sally Cripps; 111 P. Bannatyne; 113 C.D. Pay; 117 David Coventry; 118-9 Trevor Weekes; 120 David Coventry; 123 Mortlock Library; 126 Mortlock Library; 130 Australian Stock Horse Society; 134 F. Walter; 138 Lou Dowling Manns.